ONE MORE CUP OF COFFEE

WRITTEN AND ILLUSTRATED BY
Tom Pappalardo

●BJECT

OBJECT PUBLISHING
MASSACHUSETTS

ALSO BY TOM PAPPALARDO

Everything You Didn't Ask For

Failure, Incompetence

Through The Wood, Beneath The Moon
(with Matt Smith)

FIRST OBJECT PUBLISHING EDITION

OBJECT ISBN: 978-0-9983278-0-8

Book design by Standard Design

tompappalardo.com

INTRODUCTION

"For here or to go?" Jesus, I don't know. I wanted to get some work done, but it's crowded in here and the AC is cranked too high. On the other hand, I drink my coffee really slow, so maybe I need a for-here in a to-go cup. Is that a thing? It's just called a to-go? Okay, to-go.

"Do you need space?" Christ, yes. *Please.* I mean, I'm here to get out of my house, be around human beings, etc. But then as soon as I sit down, I'm annoyed and over-stimulated. Then again, I'm an observer of people. I enjoy it, I like witnessi— Oh you meant in the *cup* do I need space in the *cup.* Fuck, no. I'm paying dollar-money for this bean drink top it the fuck *off.* Make coffee goosh out the little hole in the plastic lid. Make my hand wet with excess. Fill my world wi— Oh what, now I'm in the way of the next customer? How is this my fault? Look at him, he's not even ready to ord— Yes, sure, okay. Let me just throw unconsidered handfuls of coins into the tip jar for some fucking reason. Now I'm the bad guy, sure. Great. Great.

CLEAR SKIES (SIP, NORTHAMPTON)

It's a blustery New England morning on Main Street. I inhale a chilly lungful of Monday, smug in the knowledge that, unlike west coast writers, I get to use words like "blustery." I step into SIP for a coffee and a bagel. I'm not sure if all-capping SIP is required, but I do it because I dig their sign, which is all-caps, which is successful branding.

It's an odd room, a unique aesthetic for this town. Am I in an Ikea catalog, or on a movie set for a scene involving a cafe that looks like an Ikea catalog? White walls of horizontal wood strips remind me of slat wall in a mall store. One wall is wallpapered in trees, another is chock-full of coffee-related kitchen gadgetry. The menu board has no prices on it, which is annoying. What am I, a Rockefeller? Give me facts and figures. SIP's front door features a lovely metal sign by Sam Ostroff. He's cornered the local market for handmade metal signs. They're everywhere, and he's damn good at it. On the other hand, he's the same guy who made that metal mural on the other end of Main Street, which I think is a gigantic clip art turd.

The barista is a talker, and when I tell him my name for my order, he tells me he's a Tom, too, and we have a bonding moment over that. I want to reference Vonnegut's *Slapstick*, but I can't assemble a concise description of the artificial family concept in my as-yet-uncoffee'd brain quickly enough, and the moment passes, so I don't mention it. I'm of the opinion that small talk conversations are like space shuttle launches: there are narrow windows of clear skies, and if you don't fire the boosters, you lose your chance, millions of dollars are wasted, and a bunch of astronauts get mad at you.

I sit with my small coffee. It's French press, I think? I'm not a person who pays close attention to coffee stuff. I get French press confused with French Roast and French Vanilla. Anyway, it's coffee and it tastes good, so that's good. My bagel is also good, and unlike other establishments in town, it doesn't come with a four pound slab of butter on the side. The stereo plays the theme song from *Portlandia*, which I find hilarious. Over by the trees, a man takes a photo of his latte. Is it on Twitter now, that moment in time, the brief existence of that pretty floating foam leaf? Did people favorite it and retweet it? That latte photo's probably trending right now. Trending across the goddamned planet.

There's a gray boomer slouched in the window seat watching a video on his smartphone with the volume turned way up. I'm impressed by his goatee and his earring and his cargo shorts and his Chili Challenge t-shirt. He's doing an amazing job of almost convincing people he's a laid back, totally hip non-old person. I pity him because he's so old he can't hear all the high frequencies from his phone that are stabbing my ears and causing dogs to howl a block away. I try to compliment the exquisite audio fidelity of his portable digital device by shouting across the room "THAT SOUNDS LIKE A GREAT FUN VIDEO DOES IT GO ANY LOUDER," but he doesn't even acknowledge me. Poor old dude. He can't hear me because my voice is so high and wire-thin, a balloon with a slow leak, like Willie Whistle. Poor old dude.

Including myself, there are four other white men with beards and eyeglasses and laptops camped out here. We're all writing clever things, amused by our own cleverness. When will people recognize our cleverness? Someday, we'll all be famous writers, and we'll be invited to big fancy dinner parties where we'll electrify the room with our small talk, launching rockets of conversation, resting our wine glasses on the decorative fireplace mantle as we fondly recall this blustery, blustery New England morning.

> ## "I'm addicted to cheese. I love cheese. More cheese, please."
> *– Person at next table, The Roost*

CHOPPY SMUDGE
(WOODSTAR, NORTHAMPTON)

Woodstar and I go way back, as far back as it goes. I was a customer on their opening day. I ordered a cup of coffee, and it was disgusting. Not just bad, but WRONG. I was willing to drop it in the trash and never return, but my girlfriend convinced me to say something to them. Turns out a new machine had been improperly cleaned or something. I think I drank a bit of soap. I got a replacement coffee, and it was great, and it's been great ever since. And so have the sandwiches, the bagels, and the hot chocolates. I goddamn love this place. For a stretch of time, I came here twice a day, every day, an escape from my home office.

I wait in line, aggressively desiring the blueberry muffins in the glass case. I order a coffee and a sandwich. The cashier asks me a question over the din of the cafe. "For here," I say. When my sandwich is ready, the worker calls the name "Peter," which might sort of sound like "for here" in a loud room, I guess.

I sit at a table and write in my notebook (graph paper) with a ballpoint (PaperMate) pen. I'm a lefty, so the side of my palm (the karate chop part) smudges blue ink across each line I write. A man sits next to me, typing on a miniature laptop with keys like a baby's fingernails. I swear he's peeking at my writing. Hey, you, guy. Can you read this?

IS MY WRITING BIG ENOUGH? REIN IT IN, MOTHERFUCKER.

He pretends to not notice, but I know. *Oh, I know.*

A college girl sits to my right, leaning in the corner, sideways and facing me with her laptop in her lap. She's way over the Invisible-But-Real-Cafe-Personal-Space-Line. If our genders were reversed, this would be a classic example of manspreading. Instead, I guess it's just rude, or weird, or ladyspreading. I beg the miniature laptop man to Google "ladyspreading" on his pocket calculator. A mere 188 results! I've just practically-almost-mostly coined a new stupid word! I bet the Image Search results are NSFW (Not Safe For Woodstar).

A woman monologues to her friends about how her indestructible cellphone screen got scratched. An older gentleman boasts about how un-finicky he is when it comes to sandwiches. Some kids talk about gender identity and mention "the T word." I didn't realize another word had become unmentionable beyond its first letter, but here we are. A middle-aged regular sits on the bench where customers wait to pick up orders. He's waiting to pick something up, too — probably a college girl with low self-esteem.

"Take a Look at Me Now" comes on the stereo. Phil Fucking Collins. Wait, is it called "Against All Odds," or was that a movie? Phil pounds his big reverby drums and I cease to give a shit about minor details like titles. Hell of a song, man. Overblown and overwrought and over-produced. I love it. I think more short, balding white men need their voices heard. Godspeed, Lil Phil. Heal from your emotional wounds.

I karate chop another sentence. Peter's sandwich is delicious.

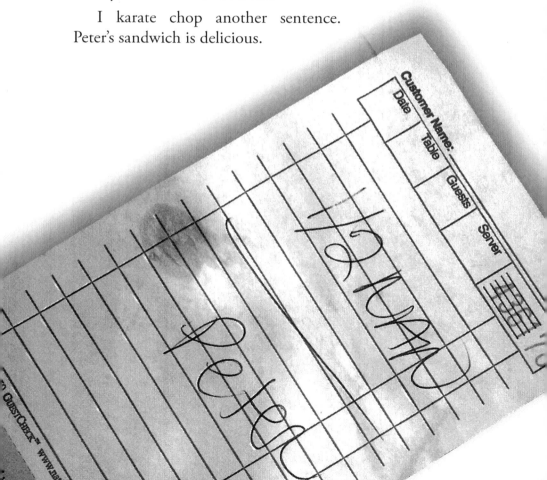

THE WAY STATION (STARBUCKS, HADLEY)

In a strip mall amongst strip malls, next to businesses with made-up sounding names like Hot Table and Sweet Frog and Sex Oven and Pizza Studio and Fresh Griddle, there is bound to be a Starbucks. There is indeed a Starbucks here, built in front of a Home Depot, right where it should be, as the Elder Ones foretold in the Ancient Book Of Zoning.

I order a small coffee and a bagel. The coffee comes in a late-2015-infamous red cup. If you don't recall what I'm talking about, well, that should give you an idea of how unimportant this thing was when it was momentarily deemed important. In my personal online bubble, the sarcastic/joke responses to the red cup war-on-xmas 'controversy' showed up before the actual story. But that's the internet in a nutshell: Outrage about a non-outrageous thing, plus outrage at the outrage, equals a thing to distract people from their complicit roles in an unjust society facing imminent collapse. Sorry. Spoiler alert.

This is a quick stop. I'm on the way to Home Depot, my new Home Depot away from home. Depot. I've been soundproofing my basement so I have a place where I can go and scream without disturbing my neighbors. I use the Starbucks bathroom on the way out. It's fantastic, straight out of the Death Star detention block. Looking in the mirror, I spy an unforgivably long nose hair escaping my left nostril. Thanks a lot, Starbucks! What the fuck. I step outside, back into the real, terrible world. The setting sun pierces the dark clouds over Chipotle, its light traveling 92.96 million miles across space just to hit me in the eye. This is the most pleasant moment of my day.

TROUBLE (LOOK RESTAURANT, LEEDS)

It's 8:30 on a Sunday morning, and I arrive at the Look Restaurant up by the V.A. Hospital. The Look used to have a great old neon sign on it. I think it got knocked off by an 18-wheeler or something a few years back. The mangled remains sat in the corner of the parking lot for awhile. A guy thought it was trash and took it. When he read an article about its theft in the *Gazette* the next day, he apologized and brought it back. They never did put it back up.

I trip on the threshold as I step inside, which could be a foreboding premonition of things to come, or it could just mean I'm sleepy. I sit at the counter without any further complications. Coffee, yes, please. It's a good, solid mug. The kind of mug you could break into a car with. The waitress wipes down my stretch of counter, and now the back of my notebook is wet. The countertop is Formica, with a microscopic dot pattern that looks more like a printing error than an aesthetic choice. It's a small room, and the morning chatter echoes off the floor tiles. The median age of the room is 62.3. I have a keen eye for things like this. Trust me. My barber sits in a corner booth with his family. He's in charge of scheduling the Florence Community Room, so he's pretty much the town equivalent of a mafia don. Only the penitent man shall pass. I kiss his ring and return to my seat.

Norm floats in and takes the corner counter stool. I know his name because everybody knows his name, like on *Cheers*, but for real. Everybody in the place says "Morning, Norm." He calls the waitress Trouble and orders a big breakfast. Norm wants to engage me in conversation. I can feel him looking at the side of my head, but I keep my eyes glued to my yolks. Trouble asks Norm how he's doing, and he launches into a monologue about trailering his friend's boat out to the Oxbow. About fishing in Norwich, and the high winds there. He has a bad shoulder. He covers a lot of bases topic-wise, and the stories continue until his breakfast arrives. Then he eats in silence at an astonishing and steady tempo. Pick up breakfast burrito, insert into mouth, put down burrito, dip a homefry in bowl of hollandaise sauce, insert into mouth, add ketchup, drink coffee, loop. One, two, three, four. One, two, three, four. It's an elaborate performance of coordination set to a rhythm buried deep in his stomach. In another life, he could've been a percussionist. In this life, he is Norm.

There's a guy sitting to my right who could have asked me to pass the pepper shaker to my left, but he instead opts to stand and grab one from an empty table behind us. I empathize. I wouldn't have asked, either. He's reading the paper, and I try to peek at the comics page out of habit. I finish my eggs and put my money and Guest Check under my empty mug, as if a strong gust of wind might blow through the restaurant and whisk my payment away before the waitress can pick it up. Or perhaps I believe a coffee mug will somehow thwart a passing thief from pocketing the cash. Basically, I'm convinced that if the waitstaff is occupied elsewhere and I leave my payment unattended, someone will shout "HEY, YOU DIDN'T PAY!" and I'll turn and the money will be gone. It's an irrational fear, like when I used to worry about being accused of stealing my own clothes out of a laundromat dryer. I am under constant surveillance. People are watching me, waiting for me to step out of line so they can judge me. So I put the goddamned mug on the goddamned money, okay?

I manage to escape to the parking lot unaccused of theft, and I don't trip on the threshold, either. It's a pretty morning. A little damp, like my notebook.

LET'S JUST AGREE IT'S JUNE 15TH
(THE FOUNDRY, NORTHAMPTON)

I order a coffee at the cash register, which is about a foot from the coffee dispenser, which is a mere ten inches away from my waiting hand. The barista pours my coffee and places my cup on a pick-up counter eight feet away. He walks back and asks me if I'd like anything else. I want to point and say "That coffee over there," but I don't.

I grab a seat, open my notebook to a blank page, and write "June 15th." Is it June 15th? I could check my phone, but I'm too lazy. Let's just agree it's June 15th. I remember when this space was The Yellow Sofa, the stupidest-named business in downtown Northampton until Shop Therapy opened. I'd never witnessed a business have an identity crisis before. Every time I visited the Yellow Sofa, something was different. First it was books and "Hey! Ceramics!" Then it was coffee and "Look! We've got greeting cards!" Then it was open mics and "Please somebody buy a baklava something anything dear god we're drowning this chair is for sale."

The Foundry's remodel of the space is fantastic. I appreciate the choices made for the walls, the tables, the counter, the floor. It's a swell room. A handwritten sign on the Foundry's front door says "Weekends are wifi-free!" with smaller text underneath that clarifies "*No wifi on weekends." I can't tell if this is supposed to be hilarious or not, but I laugh. The asterisk is the clincher. I've been sitting here for awhile. I check my phone. Ooohh, lunch break is over. And shit, it turns out it's June 17th. Huh. I take a sip of my coffee. It tastes pretty good, considering I bought it two days ago.

Woodstar Cafe: Two girls study next to me. Two laptops, two cups of water, and a burrito from Bueno Y Sano they're stealthily sharing, passing it back and forth under the table. Maybe they think they're being clever? That no one can see them? That this local business is an extension of their campus? THUMBS DOWN.

A SUFFOCATING DESPAIR
(BIG Y WORLD CLASS MARKET CAFE, NORTHAMPTON)

It takes one sip for me to definitively declare that Big Y coffee is gross. It cost $1.60. It would've only cost 78 cents had I possessed a magical silver Coin Of Savings. I connect to the supermarket's free wifi. My browser redirects to a Big Y landing page which displays a near-pornographic closeup of sliced swordfish. Journey's "Send Her My Love" melts out of the overhead speakers, interrupted by a prerecorded pitch man — his weird, friendly Keebler Elf-like voice informing customers of the seedless grape deals awaiting us in the produce section. Beguile me not, man-Siren! "You Can't Change That" comes on, which I'd always assumed was a Hall & Oates song, but a quick Google search informs me it's an early Ray Parker Jr. project called Raydio. How did I never know this?

A prerecorded dietician talks about antioxidants, and then the pitch man's voice bursts onto the PA again. This time, his voice is crunchy and robotic and plays back at the wrong speed. His sentences overlap and I can't comprehend a single word other than "wow." My guess is an improperly compressed audio file. It's seriously fucking jarring. You'd think a manager or someone would take it out of rotation, but I guess not. The workers must be numb to it. I bet it's been doing that since 2009.

I have another sip of the coffee. It has failed to become less gross. I try the blueberry muffin I bought at the bakery counter. It is, um... very blueberry-flavored? The PVTA bus pulls up and blocks the window. The room grows dark as a suffocating despair casts a shadow over my soul. Trapped! Do any locals remember the old Pioneer Valley Transit

17

Authority logo? The one in the stylized curved letters that could easily be read as "PUTA"? That, my friends, is why one pays for professional graphic design.

A chatty woman sits at a nearby booth, keeping an elderly lady company — someone she seems to have just met. She talks about family members as the older woman eats a salad. It's a skill I don't have, the ability to unselfconsciously fill silence with chatter, one I appreciate in an odd way. I consider this sort of talk to be annoying and pointless, while recognizing its function as a social lubricant. I'm sure my lack of it must make me seem too curt sometimes, too blunt. If I could communicate solely in bullet points, I would.

• No, really

The woman says her last name is Kellogg, and reveals that her high school nickname was Corn Flakes. Corn Flakes gives thanks to God for her slice of pizza. Corn Flakes talks about a friend-of-a-friend who enjoys being a nurse. She talks about training dogs and substitute teaching. Corn Flakes talks about helping veterans, Asperger's, going to church, jury duty, and her divorce. Oh boy, too much about the divorce. We hear a lot about the divorce, and I begin to sympathize with the ex-husband. The elderly lady maintains a slight smile and chews on her iceberg lettuce.

The bus moves on, the room fills with sunlight, and I notice the flag in the parking lot is at half mast. I've been doing my damnedest to isolate myself from world news these past few months, so I have no idea what terrible thing has happened. Maybe they just stay at half mast now. I could go poke around CNN's website, but I'm not going to. The insane elf/demon/Dalek announcer barks at the customers again. I take another sip of my coffee. I can't help it. When will I learn?

"Careless Whisper" plays a short time after "Father Figure." A George Michael twofer. A pretty teenage girl comes in, sits at a booth, and faffs around with her phone. I want to tell her to run away, run with great haste. Don't look back, miss! Don't let this orange/brown tomb envelop you. Don't give in and accept this place as being good enough, young blossom! You have so much to live for, so much life ahead of you still! Don't become another Corn Flakes. Don't become another me.

A second bus pulls up, filled with a malevolent darkness. My cup is still 7/8 full.

VARYING DEGREES OF ASS-HARDSHIP
(THE ROOST, NORTHAMPTON)

The Roost stands guard at one of the gateways to downtown, across from the train bridge with the painfully inoffensive river mural on it. The best feature of this bridge is that it is low and gets hit by 18-wheelers a lot, and let me assure you, this is one of the most entertaining delights Northampton has to offer. Screw the local music scene — squat on a corner of this intersection and wait for the inevitable shrieking squeal of a too-tall truck getting scalped. Then you get angry commuters, police lights, detours, road flares, and if you're lucky, pallets of orange juice stacked in the middle of the street. It is an intoxicating experience, preferable to most local singer-songwriters and their bullshit.

I enter The Roost and rearrange furniture. Not because of OCD or feng shui, but because the Roost's assortment of chairs follow a definite and quantifiable comfort hierarchy. I go for the old school desk chairs first (wooden back and ass panels, optional metal book rack between the legs). Next, there are a few light steel chairs painted in 1960s orangy-pink and mint green — sturdy and inflexible bastards. After that, the seating selection devolves into varying degrees of ass-hardship.

The room is furnished with pipes and old wood and cut glass bottle light fixtures. It's a good-looking room. I'm one of many laptoppers here; at the moment the Mac-to-PC ratio stands at 13 to 2. I'm one of the two. We all sit and type on our laptops and look at white people stuff on the internet. My coffee is hot and good, one of my favorite cups in town. On the stereo, a sensitive man softly whispers sad, haunting sadness out of his sensitive, soft, sad, haunted mouth. Come here, little bird. Let me hold you.

The young woman to my right closes her Macbook and walks away. Coffee refill, bathroom, I don't know. She walks off. There's a thing I've never been able to do, just leave my stuff at a table and trust the room. She didn't even do the "Could you watch my things?" thing, that odd verbal contract of cafes across this great land. She returns after a few minutes and her laptop is gone! *Holy shit!* As an aside, I have a cool new Macbook now. Where's the goddamned Start Menu on this thing?

It's busy in here. I watch a pink-faced man abandon

the crowded eight-person table when the five-person table becomes available. He claims exclusive rights to it, you can see it in his eyes. "A victory!" he thinks. "A coup!" he thinks. He spreads his laptop and bag across half the table, like he's planting a goddamned flag on the goddamned moon. Twenty seconds later, three pre-adolescent boys plop down on his moon and argue about when a mom is going to show up to give them a ride home. They chew loudly and drink root beers and talk too much and their legs never stop moving. Victory, sir. *Victory!*

IDLING ON MY FRO-PO

I sit on my front porch, sipping coffee from my Shady Glen mug. My neighbor, a young guy who favors camouflage pants paired with neon-bright shirts, pulls up in front of his apartment in his pickup truck. He lopes inside, leaving it idling with the driver's side door wide open. He is a man who enjoys running his engine recreationally.

I drink my coffee and write. The rumble of his engine makes my porch vibrate (not a euphemism). He returns after maybe ten minutes, animated and talking to himself. Is he talking to his Toyota? He fiddles around with stuff in the cab and in the bed of the truck for another minute, still talking, and eventually gets in and drives off. Rev-rev-rumble-rumble, lead foot it up the street and gone.

Later that morning, he pulls into his regular spot. He retrieves his son from the baby seat hidden in the shadows of the truck cab. Did that guy leave his goddamned child unattended in an idling, open vehicle on the street this morning? Did that *happen?* What the *shit?* Why would someone wear camouflage *and* safety colors?

> "The two breeds of Catholics I find most interesting are Irish Catholics and Italian Catholics."
> – *Two college girls discussing religion, The Roost*

VALENTINE'S
(TANDEM BAGEL COMPANY, EASTHAMPTON)

The psychological effect of sitting near a fireplace on a frigid February afternoon cannot be underestimated. I sit in the main room of Tandem Bagel, a flame in my vicinity, unsure if it's actually scientifically making me warmer. But it doesn't matter. I think it is, so it is.

Today is Valentine's Day, and people are wishing each other a happy Valentine's Day. Verbally, with their mouths. Apparently, people do this now. Thank you, Marketing Department, for this commercialized respite from the less-aggressively promoted Black History Month. Get your shit together, Black History Month. You need the Hallmark Bump. You need the blessing of Big Flower. Coordinate your resources with Hersheys. Maybe consider a product tie-in with Victoria's Secret? It's all about repetition, saturation, and repetition. Is there any way we can make Black History Month sexier? Maybe downplay the history part to appeal to a younger demographic? 18 to 25-year-old white males are where the disposable income is at — perhaps we could re-brand Black History to be a little more *white*. Reposition it in the marketplace to maximize exposure? Let's take a meeting over bagels and toss around some brand strategies.

I finish my coffee. "HAPPY VALENTINE'S DAY, ONE AND ALL!" I shout to the room, with tears in my eyes. I leap into the air and fly home on a giant heart-shaped box of chocolates from the clearance shelf at CVS.

FILL MY POCKETS WITH
HOMEFRIES (JAKE'S, NORTHAMPTON)

Early on a Saturday morning, Jake's is relaxed and quiet. If I sit at the counter long enough, the place will fill to capacity. Conversations will bounce off the dark wood paneling while waitresses move at full hustle, and people will queue up by the door. For now, it's me on the end stool, damp from an October rain.

No music playing, thank God. Just chatter, kitchen clanks, coffee maker hissing in the corner, forks on plates. Behind the counter, coffee filters filled with fresh grounds are stacked in plastic containers. A whole bunch of plastic containers. Jake's is prepared to serve a shitload of coffee today. I love everything about this room. I hope someday somebody holds my wake here. Lay my corpse on the marble countertop and toast to my memory with toast. Fill my pockets with homefries and chuck my casket over the dike. The end.

Twenty years ago, Jake's was my late night coffee destination, a wild and carefree time in my life when I would dare to drink coffee after 3pm. I'm not even sure if I knew Jake's was open during the day. It was a place to go after rock shows, a place to go after everything else had closed. There used to be a payphone in the back and excellent framed charcoal and ink drawings on the walls. The food used to be straightforward and cheap. It said so right on the sign: "No Frills Dining."

Nowadays, everything costs more and tastes much better. The jelly is too fancy and you need to pony up for real maple syrup. The fake stuff is out on the counter and tables, of course, which is a food service tactic I've never understood. If you're going to offer free crap with the option to upgrade, why not fill the table ketchup bottles with red paint? "The real ketchup costs extra," the waitresses would say.

I've sat here too long. The place fills up, as expected. I'm fond of my waitress and don't want to cost her any income by squatting at a counter space. I worry about these sorts of things, maybe too much. Maybe to compensate for people who don't care at all, I don't know. I pay my tab and tip as best I can and head back out into the weather, passing through the small group of people huddled near the door, waiting for a seat. I bet they've been watching me write this paragraph, whispering to each other about how I'm not actively chewing or sipping. "Die, you non-eating son of a bitch!" they seethe from the entrance. "We see you! You're DONE! WE SEE YOU!" I smile at these people as I pass by, and they smile back.

I step outside. Still raining. I'm over the age of 40, and I've just recently bought my first-ever umbrella. I walked here with it. I enjoy the sound of the rain hitting it. Reminds me of camping. But it's a nice morning, relatively speaking, in that New England winter-is-imminent sort of way, and I have my Red Sox hat on, so fuck it. I don't care about any goddamned rain.

"Oh, my! You have a gift!"
– Old woman peeking at my sketchbook as I draw a terrible picture of Burt Reynolds, Woodstar

The Roost: I'm sitting next to a first date in progress. They seem to have a lot in common, until it is revealed that the woman doesn't know who Larry David is. The man decides to tell her all about *Curb Your Enthusiasm*. He believes this to be a wise course of action. She nods a lot, her interest is 100% feigned. Abort, dude! ABORT YOUR UNREQUESTED VERBAL RE-CREATION OF A SITCOM PLOT BRO. He perseveres. Oh God. *LITERALLY CURB YOUR ENTHUSIASM BRO.*

"If your painter would learn to speak English, he'd understand what you want better."
— *Two women talking at The Haymarket*

HEAVY & BLACK (RAO'S, AMHERST)

A slow, groggy start to a Friday morning. I played a show last night at Pearl Street and have no work deadlines today, so it's a good excuse to drive over to Amherst for a cup of coffee and a muffin at Rao's. When you're self-employed and not especially motivated, 9 a.m. on a Friday can pretty much be the beginning of the weekend. You just sort of eeeaaaasssse into it.

My coffee comes in a heavy black mug, because I order it the same way. "Heavy and black," I growl at the barista.

He throws devil horns and we crank up thrash metal on the stereo and the whole room explodes in a frenzy of old-school moshing. I smash my forehead through the glass pastry case and don't feel a goddamned thing. I'm rock'n'roll dynamite and my fuse is burning at both ends, mama. No, no, okay, none of that happened. I politely ordered a coffee, and a young man gave it to me in exchange for United States Treasury-backed monetary notes, and there is jangly pop crap on the stereo. I'm sorry I lied to you.

I've always enjoyed this place. I used to spend a lot of time here, back when Scott Rao ran it, back when there was a big-ass coffee roaster thing looming in the corner of the room, back before they took over the Indian restaurant space, when the small parking lot was slightly larger, nineteen replacement restroom door locks ago. It's a swell couple of rooms.

I sit at one of the big tables, typing on the dense mat of cat hair that has accumulated on my laptop, hoping I make contact with the keyboard hidden somewhere below. The monitor offers no confirmation the words you're reading are being captured, as it is also covered in cat hair. I try to concentrate on writing, but as usual, Facebook sings her siren song to me, so tantalizingly close, just one browser tab away from this Google Doc. I wonder who's talking about me and what 100% positive things they're saying? Refresh, refresh. I share a photo of my cat and two people Like it. Acknowledgment! I am a human and I am alive on this planet right now.

Two other people share a six-seat table with me. I observe a familiar phenomenon: Customers choosing to sit as far away from other customers as possible. There's some good social science here. I wonder if someone has studied it, and how much money they spent on their study, and if someone rolled their eyes when they heard about it and said "Did we *really* need a study on *that?*" Anyway, we really need a study on that.

Everyone in the room is sealed off in their own private laptop and earbud bubbles. I sing "Cockles and Mussels" in my best drunken pirate voice. "ALIVE ALIVE-OOO!"

I crow, dropping my head between a UMASS girl's face and her iPad. She doesn't even notice me. Nobody notices, and I resist a panicky urge to post another cat photo to Facebook to re-validate my existence. I squint one eye and dance a peglegged jig across the tabletops. Oh, but they're all wrapped up in their Google Docs and their Facebooks, the ignorant fools! My parrot is an albatross and we are alone among the landlubbers. Coffee, coffee everywhere, and not a drop to drink.

The blueberry muffins here are great.

Small Oven: Two friends, both named Lisa, order lunch at the counter. A third woman waiting in line pipes up that her name is also Lisa. The three Lisas commiserate on their shared Lisaness.

Woodstar Cafe: A student sits next to me, doing some crazy math shit on her laptop. She mumbles crazy math shit under her breath. "Math math mathy-math," she whispers. Her laptop sits on top of its soft case, which used to be a total no-no, as it would cause the machine to overheat. Laptops run cooler than they used to, so I guess it doesn't matter anymore. So do whatever you want with your computer. Pour fucking coffee right into the goddamned keyboard, I don't care.

CONTENTS ARE FURIOUS
(DUNKIN DONUTS, KING STREET, NORTHAMPTON)

I pull the door open, a door covered with window decals pleading for corporate social media interaction, a door with a brightly-colored fiberglass "DD" logo for a door handle. I feel bad for this door. This is not a noble existence for a door.

It's early morning by my standards, but it sure isn't by Dunkin Donuts'. The line moves swiftly, as employees cheerfully recite "Can I help who's next please? Can I help who's next please?" We're all part of a finely-tuned consumer service machine here, and I strive to perform at above-standard levels. I speak clearly and briefly, with my money already in my hand. I order a bagel with a small microwaved egg rectangle on it (I draw the line at eating a Dunkin Donuts animal meat rectangle). I also order a medium coffee, even though I want a small, because I'm convinced the medium styrofoam cup contributes to the overall coffee-enjoyment experience. I don't tip because I don't have to. I get the hell out of the way of the machine, because the counter person is already talking past my head and taking orders from the people behind me. You don't want to get caught in the gears of this machine. You'll get ground up and added to a Snack'N'Go Chicken Wrap.

I sit at a counter and stare out the window. The view: a porn store, a nail salon, a full parking lot. I remember when that porn store opening was a big hubbub. A real hullabaloo. Neighbors were against it. Letters to the editor. Signs? Were there yard signs? Years later, it is as benign a presence on King Street as the combination Taco Bell/KFC up the way. They're both ugly things, and I don't think I know anybody who's ever set foot in either one.

My sandwich burns my fingertips, and then somehow becomes too cold to eat. The coffee, on the other hand, is furiously hot, and remains that way. I shouldn't be surprised, because it says so right on the cup: **"WARNING: CONTENTS ARE FURIOUS."** It's so hot it burns my entire esophagus. It burns through my body and my chair and the tile floor and the concrete slab the building rests on. With steady determination, the coffee burns its way through the planet's crust and mantle, where it remains so defiantly hot it burns the core of the planet, sending shockwaves through untold miles of rock and magma, causing a chain reaction of shifting tectonic plates that endangers the continued existence of this beautiful blue and green marble in space we call Earth. And I keep getting disconnected from the wifi.

Twenty years ago, this was one of the best Dunkins I'd ever been to. It had a semi-circular counter, and it had clung to the old-school brown and orange color scheme longer than the other locations, resisting the hideous gray/purple/pink rebranding of the '90s. There were big, solid booths instead of wobbly metal tables and chairs. The night shift was overseen by Nick, a Fred Flintstone-type with a mustache and a sugar-dusted cap. On his nametag, under "NICK," he had added "AT NITE" with a Sharpie. The donut baker would be in the back room, and you could watch him through a plexiglass window. There was a regular, an old guy who always wore a captain's hat, who would say the "time to make the donuts" line from the old TV ads, and everyone tolerated it. It was a magical late night refuge. Then the franchise owner laid everyone off and gutted the place. Now it's this bullshit, which looks like all the other bullshit. I still feel bad for the door.

The Roost: I sit at the window and watch drivers stopped at the intersection: A woman has an iPad in her hand before her car even rolls to a stop. A girl in a nice old Volvo looks me dead in the eye. A middle-aged guy driving a Mercedes thinks that fedoras are a good choice. Meanwhile, pedestrians stride by, packages in hand, heading towards the post office. That guy that looks like a sad potato shuffles down the sidewalk. If he's on his meds, he'll ask you for a cigarette. If he's off his meds, he'll call you a faggot.

DATE TO CHURCH
(EASTHAMPTON WINTERFEST PANCAKE BREAKFAST)

The Easthampton Winterfest Pancake Breakfast is in full swing in the Trinity Lutheran Church basement. This is the first time I've been in a church since the last funeral I attended, which I can't recall at the moment. Not too many kids here, which keeps things agreeably quiet in this cinderblock room of fluorescent lights and folding tables. The pancakes are good (blueberry!), and so is the sausage and the bacon and the coffee. They beat most of the sugar shacks around here, for sure. Good on ya, Lutherans! I overhear war stories, learn about cotton bleaching in Colrain, and hear chili contest boasting. I squint at the Ten Commandments poster across the room, hanging next to a painting of a slouching Jesus, but I can't clearly see or recall all ten of them. Thou shalt not forget to go to the optometrist.

I want seconds, but it is unclear whether that's part of the deal or not, and I'm not thrilled about asking. I wish there was a sign. If there was a sign, I wouldn't need to ask. If there were signs everywhere for everything, I would never have to talk to human people about human things. Asking for things is an underdeveloped social skill of mine, but since I covet my neighbor's sausage, I steel myself to... —YES!! Before I can stand, a guy walks over to the counter and asks if he can have seconds! The woman says of course! OF COURSE! Another minor anxiety averted by procrastination and overthinking! I swoop in line behind him. In NASCAR, this is known as drafting.

Who is religion? Why is God? These are the sort of theological questions I resolve to answer before my second paper plate of food is licked clean. To know the unknowable, to unravel the mysteries of religion — these are the true goals of community pancake breakfasts. All it takes is a healthy dose of maple syrup, the holiest of elixirs. Behold, the mighty maples rooted to the Earth, fed by the rain, powered by the sun! Like the Bible, the tree sap is changed by man: interpreted, commodified, made more palatable, and delivered with warnings of self-restraint. I propose that maple syrup is God. Religion: solved.

A STRUGGLE OF ENDURANCE
(SMITH CORNER CONVENIENCE PLUS, NORTHAMPTON)

Cripes, I've got a headache. A perfect opportunity to hit Green Street and grab some Advil and a coffee at Smith Corner Convenience Plus. I sit at the lone table, sharing it with Mass Lottery forms and two neat stacks of a book by someone named Mirza Massroor Ahmad. In front of me, I see Mini Muffins, Donettes, and Jumbo Honey Buns (which, coincidentally, was my nickname in high school). I'm surrounded by six or eight large refrigerator cases, their unseen compressors humming away in this inexplicably carpeted room, not quite drowning out Ryan Seacrest and his radio countdown of shitty songs I've never heard before and hope to never hear again. It's too warm in here, and the air smells too sweet. I am besieged by high fructose corn syrup.

The room is dim, a relief to my headached eyes. The owner notices me sitting here — possibly the first human being to ever sit at this table — and turns on two overhead fluorescent light banks for my benefit. It hurts my brain, but I say thank you. He asks me if I want water for my Advil, which, again, is very kind, but no thank you, because I have purchased this delicious cup of coffee. Which, for the record, doesn't technically reside within the generally accepted definition of the word 'delicious,' but I have a headache, so it'll do. Ugh, the lights.

This is one of the most pleasant convenience stores I've ever been in, but what does that statement *mean*, exactly? Why is this table *here?* Who *sits* at it? How long can a person withstand the white noise of convenience, the heat of commerce, the scent of consumption? Sitting at this table soon becomes a struggle of endurance. How long can I *last?*

I'm recorded by two ceiling-mounted security cameras, encoded into an ordered collection of pixels. On a hard drive somewhere, there is a document of me at this table, this mysterious island of wood veneer, hunched over my notebook, barely moving. Perhaps this video will be flagged as unusual and suspicious behavior by the government. "Why would anyone sit *there?*" a counter-terrorist analyst will wonder in his official report as he reviews the Patriot Act-obtained footage. "Subject sitting next to Muslim-y books," he'll note. There, in a top-secret NSA data farm somewhere in Utah, I'll spin at 7,200 rpms forever, this moment and this location inextricably timestamped to my life, part of my permanent file. This headache will become evidence and this coffee will become a crime, as my oppressors cross-examine me during my inevitable secret trial.

CUP OF JOE (TRADER JOE'S, HADLEY)

The microwave dings. I stand next to a high-traffic Employees Only door, sipping my shot glass-sized cup of free coffee, while middle-aged women graciously smash their shopping carts into each other to line up for the latest round of free sweet potato home fries samples. The girl behind the samples counter can't keep up with the snack demands of the weekend crowd. The microwave dings. I crush my body into a floor display to get out of the way of shoppers and employees. Everyone is so polite here. They're going to kill me. We share the same values. The microwave dings. I swear I'll bring a reusable bag next time.

IMPERSONATOR SYNDROME
(CUP AND TOP, FLORENCE)

Cup and Top is conveniently located in downtown Florence, on the opposite corner from that pizza place, a few doors down from that other pizza place, less than a block from those other two pizza places. There's a toddler shrieking in the rear play area, which is one of this establishment's main features (the shrieking). I order a small coffee and sit, enjoying the view of the big hole in the ground where the Exxon station used to be. There's a lot of activity over there, and a construction dude keeps darting into the main intersection, attempting to read manhole covers between passing cars. What's he looking for? Sewer? Electric? Telephone? Mutant Ninja Turtle™?

A man and a woman sit behind me, on a blind coffee date. His small talk quickly descends into an extended monologue about how unrealistically gun violence and psychopaths are portrayed in movies. Then he dives into an in-depth critique of the *Batman* franchise. Now he's talking about meeting Robert DeNiro and Jack Nicholson imposters at the Big E ("Imposters," he says. Not "impersonators." She does not correct him). Has he noticed his tablemate hasn't spoken a word in almost ten minutes? I have. I have many insights into things other people do wrong. I am a valuable, untapped resource for such observations, if only people would take advantage. I should start an advice column called "Tom, What Did I Do Wrong Now?" The man keeps talking, sharing too many smartphone photos of the imposters. It's been nearly fifteen minutes now, and she's only peppered in a few scant "mm-hmmms." This is a terrible thing to earwitness.

I seem to be perpetually disappointed with Cup and Top's coffee, and yet I end up here, due to a mixture of poor memory, hope, and convenience. I feel mean writing that Cup and Top's coffee is outright bad, but it sort of pretty much absolutely is. It's weak and tastes like an old plastic coffee dispenser. This coffee is so weak, I want to impertinently stride into its dojo and bring dishonor upon its master with my modern style of kung fu. If you were to type "weak" into Google Street View, your search result would be a photo of me, with a blurred-out face, standing on the side of the road holding this cup of coffee. If Marlboro Country is where the flavor is, then Mm-hmmm Lady, The Joker Aficionado, and I are in a different country, and all the signs say "Prohibido Fumar." If a robot from the future were to time travel to this moment to assassinate me to prevent me from writing an advice column that would eventually destroy the human race, its targeting system would lock onto the coffee cup in my hand and identify it as my weakest point. Simply put, I'm a mean person, and this isn't a very good cup of coffee.

I toss my mostly-full cup in the trash and head out into the afternoon. Everyone in town thinks about pizza, because everything smells like pizza. I catch myself inspecting manhole covers as I walk back to my car. Jeez, I could use a cup of coffee. Maybe I'll go to Cup and Top.

> ## "I'm not restrained by color."
> *— People talking about clothes, The Roost*

LIQUID GOLD
(SHELBURNE FALLS COFFEE ROASTERS, EASTHAMPTON)

Headachy and under-caffeinated, I slouch into Shelburne Falls Coffee Roasters after an icy October afternoon working on my house. It's the sort of cold where you hit your finger with a hammer, but don't realize how bad it is until you get inside and warm up. So anyway, my finger hurts. I order a bagel sandwich, and I like it just fine. The coffee is just fine, too. This place, in general, is just fine. It inspires me to go elsewhere when possible, but I never mind if I end up here. The front room is sunny, with limited table options. The back room (which I didn't realize existed for many years) is a pleasant and dark sitting area, with crappy second hand furniture on a wildly uneven floor.

I sit and install updates on my aging HP laptop. All of you Mac people are scoffing at me. I know, I know. Your magic-machines do everything right all the time and never fail and poop liquid gold into your mouths. I get it. We get it. Everyone gets it. I write while progress bars fill in. I realize two things about the name of this place: 1. I usually forget to include the word "Falls" when I say the name out loud, and 2. It turns out I have no idea how to spell "Shelburne." I keep leaning towards "Shelbourne" (as in *Identity*) while my computer wants to auto-correct it to "burnisher." A woman in too-high high heels waits for her order. She clops across the interlocking wood-esque floor panels, unsure of her balance. There's a singer/songwriter guy playing on the stereo, and I wish I knew who he was so I could avoid him for the rest of my life. It sounds as if he picked up a guitar for the first time ever in the recording studio, and the producer captured his inaugural attempt at forming chords. A man walks in and can't figure out where to stand to order. He asks if the coffee is just coffee-flavored. He tells a loud joke complaining about how everything is pumpkin-flavored, like we're all audience members for his talk show monologue. Looks like we've got a real Leno here.

I'm pleased this place doesn't smell like the SFCR location on King Street in Northampton, which reeks of vanilla to such a degree that I can't physically enter the room. Or at least it did the last time I attempted to cross the threshold, which might've been two decades ago. I hate the smell of vanilla. I hate candy stores and candle stores, too. If I ever commit suicide, I'll do it at the Yankee Candle hellscape up in South Deerfield, which I imagine smells like all three things in unbearable quantity. I'll impale myself on a miniature New England village display or some shit.

I reboot my laptop. It poops liquid gold into my mouth. Take THAT, Steve Jobs' ghost!

DOWN IN THE PRIUS HOLE
(QUARRY CAFE, RIVER VALLEY MARKET, NORTHAMPTON)

It's early on a Monday morning at River Valley Market, and the workers and customers and cash registers are still waking up. I manage to do three things wrong during the simple twenty-second checkout transaction. *Which way does the stripe go? Wait, this is the wrong credit card. I'm sorry, my pants are caught in the conveyer belt thing.* I sit in the Quarry Cafe with a coffee and a muffin. The coffee's all right. I fear the compostable coffee cup lid will start composting before I finish my drink. The gluten-free blueberry muffin is acceptable, except now I just want a bunch of gluten to balance everything out. That's just how I roll. I bought lunch from the hot bar for later, and it ended up costing me $10.71. I'm not good at shopping by the pound, especially when I'm hungry. Everything looks good under a cough shield, ya know?

I stare out the window, because there's nothing else to stare at. The Priuses create mesmerizing patterns in the parking lot, which is carved out of an old stone quarry. I don't mean to over-focus on a liberal stereotype, but seriously, there are a shitload of Priuses here. Maybe this is the quarry where Priuses are mined from. An ad on my table promotes a workshop on natural medicine and an earthen oven construction class. My laptop can't connect to the wifi, forcing me to sit and write and pay attention and experience the present moment. How infuriating.

I shuffle back to my car with my lunch and a bag of coffee beans (I have a bag of salted peanuts, too, but let's save that for my next book, *One More Sack Of Nuts*, coming Summer 2021). I exit along the high rock wall and wait five hundred years for a chance to take a non-suicidal right turn onto North King Street. By the time I'm able to safely pull into traffic, I've run out of gas, deeply regretting not owning a Prius.

"You work here?"
- Old guy speaking to a Dunkin Donuts employee, a young woman who is wearing a Dunkin Donuts uniform and is standing behind the Dunkin Donuts counter, inside a Dunkin Donuts

Tandem Bagel: A high school boy waiting in line towers over me. I'm not a person accustomed to being towered over, so I need to mention it every time it happens, the way some people are compelled to tell you about a dream they had that you don't give a shit about. I need to verbalize it to process it. "Did you see that guy?" I'll say, my voice full of wonder. "He's like six-seven, fer chrissake." A woman speaks snippily into her phone, and then adds "I don't mean that snippily." A little kid throws himself onto the red couch. Children love to chuck their bodies at this couch. It's a little body magnet. The woman sitting next to me turns away from her bagel to sneeze. Onto mine, basically.

Haymarket: A guy sits down with a Murakami book. I want to ask him about it, even though I haven't read it myself, because I like what Murakami I've read. But this guy is busy reading and he's a stranger and I wouldn't have much of anything to add to the conversation that would ensue if I were to bother him. You can't interrupt someone who's reading just so you can acknowledge that you like reading, too. That's goddamned crazy. "How's that sandwich taste?" asked the sociopath. "Man, I love sandwiches!" This is one of the many reasons why I don't make friends too easily. Small talk makes me want to kick my own head off. "How's that book?" Jesus Popsicle Stick Christ, Tom.

THE ALARMOLYPSE
(THE DONUT MAN, HADLEY)

The Donut Man looks like a BayBank branch that closed in the '80s filled with a bunch of discarded fixtures from an old Dunkin Donuts. Their styrofoam cups are also quite Dunkin-y, and their logo is an illustrated pink frosted donut with sprinkles, which appears to be stolen from *The Simpsons Movie* poster. According to their business card, there are four The Donut Man locations: three in western Massachusetts, and one in Myrtle Beach, South Carolina. I guess we know where the owners spend their winters.

I'm sitting in one of those seats — not a booth... y'know, those things where it's two small tables welded together with four spinny chairs attached to a steel frame?

One of those. I'm sitting at one of those. "At that"? I can't even tell if this goddamned leg-constricting cage is singular or plural. Anyway, I'm in one of thems, next to the fireplace (yes, there's a fireplace), facing the side of a refrigerator case full of soda. My view is dominated by a human-sized Pepsi bottle graphic that appears to be so cool and bold and refreshing, it's downright aggressive.

The donuts (or "doughnuts" if you have an overabundance of time, and choose to type out every useless letter ever invented) at The Donut Man are all good, or at least I assume they're all good. See, I'm always on the lookout for a great granulated sugar jelly donut (NOT POWDERED, YOU FOOL), and The Donut Man has a great granulated sugar jelly donut. One of the best I've had in the Pioneer Valley. It's so great, I haven't bothered with any of their other donuts. So based off my knowledge of *this* donut (the one in my mouth, right now, as I write), I will assume all the other donuts are at least pretty good, too.

The woman working the register leans over the side of the counter and speaks to a man who has walked in and sat at a booth without ordering. She has a great accent, I'm guessing Jamaican.

HER [STERN]: "Do you need anything else?"

HIM: "What? Me?"

HER: "Do you need anything else?"

HIM [CONFUSED AND GUILTY]: "I'm just using the wifi."

HER: "Ten dollars."

HIM: [FLUSTERED SOUNDS]

HER: "Ha-ah-ha, I'm kidding! You looked so serious!"

Every time the door opens, a shrill digital chime bleats behind the counter. There's also something else beeping back there, maybe a loud coffee maker or a quiet smoke detector? None of the workers seem too motivated to shut it off. Security system? Drive thru notification? Is a convoy of tractor trailers about to back up through the wall? I'm ready to stick cinnamon buns over my ears like Princess Anne-Droid when the alarmolypse finally ceases.

Across the room, an older guy chews on a danish. Based on his hat, scarf, and coat, I'm guessing he's either a fancy hobo or a Victorian-era chimney sweep (I mean, in my defense, he's covered in soot *and* has a bindle, so it's hard to say for sure.) A television is tuned to FOX or CNN or something else annoying. A mom and a dad try their damnedest to ignore their crying toddler. We are all being watched by an abundance of security cameras.

A partially deaf Latino woman asks me where the court is. This is the perfect storm of my insecurities: being asked for directions by someone who isn't speaking clearly and also can't hear me. But I figure out the question after only asking her to repeat it once, and unbelievably, I know she means the courthouse AND I know where the courthouse is. I ANSWER HER QUESTION CORRECTLY. This is a big success for me. I sit back in my eating-cage, covered in sugar, savoring this social victory. Come celebrate with me! Let us eat jelly donuts together!

NOT POWDERED.

Woodstar Cafe: A woman fiddles with the water dispenser on the counter. She tilts it this way and that, informs a worker that she thinks it might be empty, and leaves. Some people talk like that, softening certainties with "I thinks" and "mights" and "maybes." We need more declarative statements in our society, like "This is empty" or "You have a massive poop stain on the ass of your skinny jeans." The woman leaves the dispenser's spigot open, and when the worker goes to refill it, water gooshes all over the floor. A bro from New Jersey walks up to the register. He is wearing a baggy gray sweatsuit. "Lodge Ice Coughy," he says.

THE OGRE (WESTERN WOODS COFFEE,
TUESDAY FARMER'S MARKET, NORTHAMPTON)

I show up at Northampton's weekly farmer's market early — early enough that nobody will sell anything until one of the organizers rings a bell. Tables of fresh produce fill the area between Thorne's and the parking garage, as patient customers mill around on this lovely mid-November afternoon. When the bell is rung, a plague of locavores descend upon the harvest like a ravenous pack of Pavlov's dogs. I am proud and horrified by the preceding sentence. What's done is done.

I wait in line to buy a cup of coffee from the Western Woods table. This guy is selling Guatemalan coffee, so I don't quite get why he's vending at a locally-focused farmer's market, but it's a thing that's allowed by the bell-ringers, in the same way a Ford with a Hyundai-built chassis and a Mazda-built engine is allowed to be called an American car because of where it's assembled. In front of me, there's an old guy in line asking why the coffee is so expensive. He ain't kiddin': $4.00 for a small cup of hot bean water. The pour-over setup is a bit much, too. Copper pipes and fancy glass filter-holders and little water pots, just a few tarnished gears away from being a steampunk top hat. It's charming enough, I guess, but I gotta tell ya, if I wasn't writing this damned thing, I wouldn't spend $4.00 on a wee cup of coffee. I should ask for a handcrafted, artisanal receipt so I can write this off. After my pour over finally pours over, I get my cup of coffee. No lid, but sure, it's good. It's a fine cup of coffee.

I claim a few feet of public bench. Some of these moms are straight-up killing it right now. Yoga pants, my dear lord. The expensive wood-fired pizza smells delicious. I want to put it in my face, along with the expensive maple syrup and the expensive bread. Possibly all at once. Two little boys play hide and seek with their mother by crawling under a park bench and screaming as loud as they can. She feigns confusion. "Where are they?" she calls out. "Where could the boys be?" The boys shriek "Chase us!" and she does. They shriek "Freeze!" and "Unfreeze!" and she does and she does. I appreciate her ability to play along. I'm not particularly adept at playing along. I'm trying to get better at it, but kids just don't seem to respond to my dead-faced sarcasm, the little fucking shits. I want to swing a gigantic brussel sprout stalk like an ogre's battle axe and chase them away. BEGONE, SCREECHIES.

I saw Bob Mould rock Tuesday Market a couple of years back. A five or six song set, part of a radio promotion for a Pearl Street show, I think. It was a disappointing turnout — I was one of maybe four people who knew who he was or cared he was rocking out next to some beets, giving an almost soundcheck-worthy performance. I was demoralized and disappointed on his behalf, but then again, I didn't go to his show that night, so I guess I'm the asshole, right?

I've enjoyed this beverage and this little slice of my community, but now my coffee's cold, I need both hands to carry lettuce and my new battle axe, and this goddamned cup didn't come with a goddamned lid. I throw away around $1.50's worth of locally-imported caffeine. I take a final inhale of delicious pizza-air and think about the cheap Stop & Shop-sourced sandwich I'll hand-craft when I get home. We're all local heroes, in our own way.

At the Bluebonnet Diner while my tires are aligned up the street. I sit in front of the pie case, which triggers a deep desire for diner pie. It's not the greatest pie. My logical mind knows this. But it isn't *bad* pie. It's *pie*. I resist all pie case temptation and order a coffee and a cheeseburger club. It's a difficult sandwich to eat tidily or slowly. It's a shove-it-in-your-mouth-before-it-falls-apart sort of scenario. I create a medium-sized lake of tomato-flavored high fructose corn syrup on my plate for an easy french fry dippin' good time. Umami in full effect. I want them pie case pies. I see you, you sumsabitches. Imma come an' git you.

DULL AND UNFOCUSED
(PANERA, HADLEY)

Too early in the goddamned morning and I'm up and I'm in my car and I'm driving to Hadley. I wanted to go to Barnes and Noble to look at books I wasn't planning on buying, to wander around with dull and unfocused eyes. But I arrive at the old mall plaza an hour before the bookstore opens, so now I'm here, at the Panera next door.

Everything about the Panera experience is focused on efficiency. I stand alone in a vast open area where lines form during peak hours, next to a big shelf for picking up online orders. There are seven workers behind the counter, yet it still takes five minutes for someone to wander over to the register to take my money. Coffee and a bagel. The coffee dispensers are labelled with the time when the coffee was brewed, which doesn't matter because it tastes horrible. The dark roast says 6:30 on it, I'm just not sure what day. You know how some places make iced coffee by recycling the old hot coffee and it tastes kinda gross? This tastes like that, if the old iced coffee was then recycled back into hot coffee again.

So I'm not in a bad mood per se, but I'm tired and cold and grumpy and I'm not being caffeinated the way my human adult body sometimes requires. I'm sitting somewhere I don't want to be, drinking weakness. I'm unwilling to change my situation, as that would require me to go back outside. So I huddle in the corner, wearing my coat, sitting next to the not-turned-on fireplace, because it's winter and this Panera has a frickin' gas fireplace but the thing isn't turned on. I view this lack of desire to improve my state of being through action as a moral failing on my part.

The wifi drags its feet. Maybe the three retirees reading the New York Times on their phablets are sucking bandwidth, I don't know. Or maybe my laptop needs to warm up — it's a friggin' aluminum ice cube under my palms. An old man inches towards the trash barrel, taking halting, wide-stance steps. He's either got a hip problem, or he's wearing a laundry basket as a diaper. "Your bagel's ready at the next counter," a worker tells a customer waiting near the registers. The next counter is half a mile away.

"HEY, BABY. SMILE!" I shout at a pretty girl sitting near the door, because I've read on the internet that women enjoy this sort of thing. I cement my male dominance of this space, this terrible space with its terrible coffee and its terrible swirly-pattern commercial carpeting. I can barely discern her emotional compliance through all the smoke from the fire I've just started in the fireplace. I stuffed it full of cups and napkins and hair. Fuck it. Burn it. Burn everything. This coffee is terrible.

THE STAND
(TART BAKING COMPANY, NORTHAMPTON)

I'm standing underneath a fantastic light fixture in the front window of Tart Baking Company. "Standing?" you ask. "But, Tom, you hate standing. Standing is for losers." I know, dear reader. It's true. Tart is one of those awesome places that doesn't offer any chairs, just two counters and a standing-height table. I might sound like I'm being sarcastic, but I'm not. I appreciate business owners who aren't afraid to push their customers out the door. I still sound sarcastic, but I'm still not. So I'm standing here, writing in a notebook. I sense that maybe nobody wants me to be doing this, but I'm doing this.

The dark roast here is very dark and very roast, and this raspberry muffin is super good. Not as good as the aforementioned light fixture — a beautiful bundle of paper-thin wood sheets with a light bulb jammed in the middle — but still quite tasty, and much less likely to cause an electrical shock and/or lip splinter if bitten into.

I gaze upon beautiful downtown Northampton, surely one of the best views of Main Street to be had, or at least it would be if it wasn't for Tart's gigantic, low-hanging, red and white striped awning which blocks the entire view. I'm 6'3" and standing on a raised platform three steps above street level, so all I can see besides inner-awning is a bit of sidewalk and the front end of a Honda Element. Passing pedestrians look up and are confronted by a giant pale man behind glass, his crotch at eyeball level, staring down at them from up under a circus tent. A carnival barker points at me with his cane and crows "WHY, LADIES AND GENTS, THE GHASTLY GIANT DRINKS FROM CUPS JUST LIKE YOU AND ME!"

An old white guy who drives the front end of a Lexus walks in. He's wearing a blue blazer and tan slacks. "Hi! How are you?" the counter person asks. "Thank you!" he replies. I love this sort of exchange: a question asked so the answer can be ignored, followed by an answer which ignores the question. This is polite banter in our society, the equivalent of a security question on your bank's website, except it doesn't matter if the name of your first pet was Thundercat or if your mother's maiden name was Dicktard. Just say whatever, and it's fine.

I've been here awhile now, longer than the average customer. I'm tempted to lean forward and rest on my elbows, but I can see the large, invisible No Slouching sign on the wall. The staff cranks the air conditioning up in an attempt to drive me out. But I *refuse!* Do your worst, Tramplers-Of-Rights! Anti-Seatists! Hip-Breakers! Upright Gestapo! I WILL PREVAIL AND PROSPER HERE AT THIS COUNTER AND I SHALL OVERCOME YOUR MICRO-AGGRESSIONS BY STANDING IN SOLIDARITY WITH MYSELF.

On the sidewalk below, a young lad in short-pants throws peanut shells at me and correctly guesses my weight. I award him a stuffed pink elephant and head home.

The Roost: I sit next to a couple who maintain finger-touching contact while talking — a sweet, intimate thing in stark contrast with their dead-boring conversation about mediocre television and forgettable movies. I manage to eat a Market Street Salad without launching lettuce all over the table. A college girl in a short pleated skirt and knee socks keeps distracting me by standing and shifting her weight from one foot to the other. *Can't she see I'm pretending to write?* A few seats down, a guy knits, which isn't all that notable, except he also looks prepared to kick everyone's ass for any number of reasons, including "no reason at all."

WHY AM I UP (STABLES, HADLEY)

I was out late last night, til 1:30 a.m., hamburgers with friends, strangers, and minor television personalities. Since I went over my regular zero-beer limit and my apartment is an arid death kiln, I awake at 5:30 feeling mummified, yet frighteningly alive. I feed the cat in the dark, and I'm in my car before the streetlights have turned off. I need someone to hand me a mug of coffee and a plate of food, because I'm too tired to comprehend the assembly and construction of these things, though it appears I'm able to throw 3,000 pounds of steel down the road no prob. Such is the American psyche. I aim the vehicle towards Stables in Hadley, because every previous attempt to visit this place has been foiled by either long lines or non-openness. I figure this is my chance. I am correct.

I grab the end counter stool, away from the drafty door. The coffee is just what I need — it is hot and it is black and it is good. The waitress comes by and I order the Club Breakfast. She asks me how I'd like my eggs. I can visualize over easy, but can't quite form the phrase with my head brain and mouth hole. I mumble something and she decodes it, which is how you know you've got a good waitress. While I wait to get clubbed, I sip my coffee and read the placemat ads. I'll never understand why real estate agents (not to be confused with Realtors®, who are trying like hell to not end up like frisbees in dumpsters) insist on putting their faces in their ads. I mean, I understand the marketing angle, but Lord, some of these people would be better served with clip art.

Pop country on the radio. A waitress misuses the word "sext" while joking with a customer. I get my food (the homefries!), and a minute or so later, my check. I approve of this. I mean, if the place was packed, I'd worry I was being ushered out the door. But it's quiet, and it's okay, and I can stop projecting manipulative emotions all over the waitstaff.

"No golf today?" a manager asks a customer walking in the door. It's a joke, because it's 18 degrees out, but the man replies "10:30." Don't get me started on golf, seriously. It's too early and I'll just get grumpy and I'm actually in a pretty good mood. The only good thing to come out of the game of golf is *Caddyshack*. I mean, I guess *Happy Gilmore* was okay at the time.

Down the counter, a guy's phone plays music. An alarm, maybe. He kinda takes his sweet time silencing it. That's the sort of thing I'd jump on if it was me. Everybody has the pleasure of listening to his trebly dance bullshit clash with the crap on the radio while he *sloooowwwwly* picks up his phone and hits the silence button, real casual-like. Come on, guy-two-stools-down. Shape the fuck up.

I look out the window. There are no lines painted on the barely-paved lot. When I arrived, cars were lined up along the building. I was afraid to start a second row of parking, because I feared I'd mess it up. I put my car way off to the side. Now someone's gone ahead and started the second row, and boy, they blew it. Didn't leave enough aisle. There'll be weird parking problems for the rest of the day, I bet. The die is cast! Not my fault, man.

All of a sudden, I'm super-sleepy. It's around 8 a.m., and my late night out has caught up with me. I get back in my car, close my eyes, and drive home.

EASTHAMPTON, HUH
(SMALL OVEN, EASTHAMPTON)

Last night I was in Easthampton for a rock show at Abandoned Building Brewery. Had a nice cocktail at Galaxy, too. This morning, I'm back in Easthampton to hit up Small Oven for a cuppacawffy. I lived in Easthampton thirteen years ago, but aside from the Brass Cat and Flywheel, the town didn't do much for me. These days, it's chock full of stuff to do and places to go: Luthier's Co-op, Comics N More, Coco, Sonelab, Platterpus Records, Tandem Bagel. Good ol' Easthampton. You go, girl.

I sit at the big table. It wobbles, but I'm sitting alone, so maybe it won't matter. Pixies on the stereo and red tile on the floor and Scout Cuomo art on the walls. Scout is a local artist whose work I enjoy very much, which is a statement I don't make very often. I wish she would paint goldfish on old windows for eternity. Most of the customers in line are namechecked by the staff, so I guess there are a lot of regulars coming through. I've seen three acquaintances, which is more familiar faces than I run into on an average Northampton coffee-sit. Saw a bunch of folks I knew last night, too. Hmmm. Maybe this is where all my Northampton friends disappeared to. If I see a fourth person I know, I'll move here.

The coffee is good. Atomic Coffee from Salem, Massachusetts, the infamous New England town known for the Salem Bitch Trials, where fearful townsfolk accused women of practicing bitchcraft. I want my free refill, because it's implicit in any free refill offer that one has already paid for the refill, so to not take advantage of the offer is essentially taking money out of one's pocket and throwing it into a pothole on Union Street. This place was bustling when I first got here, then it was dead-quiet for a while, and now it's bustling again. Bustling is one of those words I just don't use enough. I've used it three times in the last two sentences, though, so I'm done with it for awhile. It felt great while it lasted. Morrissey is on the stereo now, or maybe it's the Smiths. I've never cared enough to differentiate, which is but one example of why I was such an invaluable music store employee back in my day.

A fourth person I know has just walked in. Two paragraphs ago, I made an offhand comment to you, the reader, about moving here. This is equivalent to an unbreakable sacred vow, so now I've got to move to Easthampton. Shit. I mean, I'm sure it'll be great, but now I need to find a bunch of cardboard boxes. Ugh, and switching over cable. I bet my cat's gonna be pissed. Hmm, I've never broken a lease before. Ah, well. A deal's a deal. I need to change my driver's license, right? Who do I know with a pickup truck?

A fifth acquaintance walks in. *Son of a witch!*

"I feel like I have an arid landscape inside me."

— Young woman at the Haymarket who wants to write a novel or a biography about an old jazz singer, or maybe she wants to be an actress, she isn't sure yet, but she isn't worried.

SWEETIE GETS HIS BACON
(THE MISS FLORENCE DINER, FLORENCE)

Well, here I am, Miss Flo's. I barely know the waitresses anymore, but they still call me sweetie and hon and all that other bullshit young women in foodservice tend to say to endear themselves to customers. It's shorthand for friendliness: easy, economical, and ugly. It is the vinyl siding of social interaction.

I order breakfast at the counter. It's a giant slab of pinkish-gray marble and quite un-dinery, the result of a questionable renovation a decade or so ago. The cheap veneer ceiling panels that have since bubbled up were part of that mess, too. This building is a patchwork of old and new, and all the old is fantastic, and all the new is a compromise in quality. I'm critical of the little details because I love this place, I really do. Twenty-odd years of eggs and coffee and tiny flat hamburgers.

I was at Miss Flo's the night Ina retired. She was an 85-year old waitress who worked here for forty years. A local TV crew came out and everything. I remember when the cash register was by the door. I remember when the grill was at the end of the counter, and you could sit and watch your eggs get cooked and shoot the shit with the grill guy. In general, I think I remember this place better than I remember my childhood.

I spent the morning of 9/11 here. I'd gone to work, where my boss and I realized we weren't going to have a productive day. I didn't want to go home to my depressing Easthampton apartment, so I ended up at Flo's. I sat in a booth, and after she took my order, my waitress Dee sat down with me. We sighed a lot and shook our heads a lot. Dee's a wonderful woman. I haven't seen her much recently. I'm afraid to ask anyone about her.

For the first time in my life, I feel I have too much bacon on my plate. Proportion-wise, I mean, in relation to the eggs and toast. I'm a proportional eater. I prefer to sample all of my food items in turn, a bit at a time. I work my way around the plate and end the meal with a final bite of everything. I bet there's a fantastic Japanese word for this. Today, I'm faced with extraneous bacon. I eat it. Problem solved.

The Roost: I sit back and watch a couple roam the cafe, hunting for electrical outlets. I could tell them there aren't any, but it's more fun to watch the little flame of hope in their eyes sputter and die, like their laptop batteries. A guy takes a photo of his Spiderman socks and posts it to Instagram. In the corner, a little girl assesses a Chutes and Ladders game board. She studies it with the seriousness of a ship's navigator. Her brother kneels on the floor, spreading off-brand Jenga pieces all over the goddamned place. The lady next to me asks if I know what the wifi password is. I don't remember exactly, because it was saved in my laptop forever ago. "A bunch of asterisks?" I venture. She is not amused by my hilarious joke.

THE ROGERS (MCDONALD'S, NORTHAMPTON)

This starts off as a bad idea. The morning after a wet snowstorm, I decide to walk up the unshoveled bike path to McDonald's on King Street. It's a tough slog along the train tracks, past the scraggy bit of trees where some of our city's homeless camp out. By the time I reach the parking lot, my boots and socks are soaked through. I am both chilled and overheated. These discomforts — plus my magical middle class ability to forget all about those pesky homeless people I mentioned two sentences ago — make a McDonald's breakfast all the more delicious and wonderful.

I order an Egg McMuffin™, a hash brown, and a coffee. The cashier checks my ten dollar bill with one of those counterfeit pens, which I find remarkable enough to remark upon. The muted TV plays an entertainment segment about *Friends*, which is fitting since I don't think I've sat in a McDonald's since the 1990s. Nearby, a round little man sits in a booth with his newspaper and his mustache. A few booths down, three guys talk about snowmobiles, while a guy who looks like he just lost a pillow fight watches videos on his phone with the volume turned way too high. A loud Jamaican guy keeps trying to engage the workers in friendly banter. He loiters around the registers and calls one female worker Goorrrrgeous. When he tries to talk to an older white couple eating at a nearby booth, the husband terminates the conversation with a terse "Well, good luck with that." On the overhead speakers, a string of upbeat, inspirational songs pound an insistent drumbeat of positivity. I absorb lyrics like "Follow your dreams" and "Ain't no stoppin' us now" and "When I find out who I am / I'm gonna know just what to do." I'm gonna go out on a limb and say that no one in this room is following their dreams, everyone is fully stopped, and no one cares about finding out who they am.

My coffee is nothing special, but it's hot and acceptable. The Egg McMuffin™ and hash brown, which are perfectly engineered to deliver a consistent and satisfying consumer mouth experience, do exactly that. I inhale them, contemplating a re-order before I've even finished chewing my egg-pod. That's 1,090 milligrams of sodium and 450 calories in my belly already, according to the dense, tiny-text spreadsheet of nutritional information on the back of my tray liner. I don't normally pay attention to this type of data, so it doesn't mean much to me. Hell, I don't even know how much I weigh.

I need to ask at the register for sugar packets. I have

vague memories of condiments being out by the drink machines for the taking, but I guess not anymore. This policy change probably happened a decade ago. Forgive me, I'm trying to ketchup HA HA HAHAHA ha ha please, please forgive me oh god why did I do that forgive me.

There are little half walls dividing the dining area, topped with fake flower boxes full of fake plants. Hidden behind a half wall, I discover a round little man who looks a lot like the other round little man I already mentioned, except this one has no mustache. Perhaps time has fractured and I'm seeing two versions of the same person living out two possible presents. Maybe one is happy with his life, one sad. Maybe one drives a Chevy, the other, a Toyota. Married/single. Fulfilled/restless. Dresses left/dresses right. These two versions of Roger (trust me, he's a *total* Roger) parted ways and traveled their own roads, one paved in mustaches, one not. They have lived their separate lives for fifty-odd years, and now Fate has decreed their paths almost cross, here, in this McDonald's on King Street, with me as the sole witness. The two Rogers chew on their breakfasts, separated by a screen of plastic plants, unaware their one common passion has brought them so close to reconnecting: Glorious, delicious, enchanting salt.

> ## "I'm buying a cookie for the elevenses I have at 4:00."
> *– Woman in line at Small Oven*

IT WASN'T ME!
(AMHERST COFFEE, AMHERST)

Sitting at the big table at Amherst Coffee, two young men ridicule football fans. "As if they have agency in the outcome!" muses one of them, a be-scarfed and be-vested college-aged fellow of infinite bemusement. A giant woman enters the room. She's got to be seven-foot-something, even slouching. "Goddamn," I say, hopefully not out loud, but maybe. Two stylish French guys sit across from me. I'm 99% positive they're talking about me, judging my shirt, which is so wrinkled it looks like I left it in the bottom of a clothes hamper for three months, which is exactly what happened.

I step into Amherst Coffee's lovely restroom, which smells like farts. Well, poop, more likely. General butt smells, you know. This is not an indictment of the staff's cleaning ability, I'm just saying someone was in there, and, you know. Butt smells. So anyway, I don't like it. Not just for the obvious reason, but because I'm already imagining opening the door to leave and being confronted by a seven-foot-tall woman waiting to use the restroom. "IT WASN'T ME!" I'll want to shout up at her, a sure sign of guilt. I'm doomed, basically. In the mirror, I see a booger in my mustache and reassess the French situation.

Returning to the main room, I move to a front window seat, near the whiskey bar I've never had whiskey at. Across the street, there's an old dog resting her head on the edge of an SUV's open window. She seems to be staring right at me, but she's monitoring the last place she saw her owner, who's in the cafe picking something up. This dog right here is a calm old hound, no bullshit. She ain't gonna bark or jump outta no damned window. She's gonna take it *reeeaaal* easy, maybe lie down and take a nap if this errand takes much longer. This dog is living life at the proper speed. You could learn from this dog, I mean it.

The uncoolest car on the planet, a 1995 Ford Contour, pulls into a parking space in front of the cafe. It's a tan four-door sedan with brown pinstripes. It has been AutoZoned to death, the victim of multiple attempts at aftermarket uniqueness: non-stock rims, window tint, flat black rear spoiler, license plate frames, and tinted plastic rain guards clipped to the side windows. The driver has his collar up. When the four horsemen of the apocalypse ride across this wretched land, they'll all be driving tan Ford Contours.

I drink my dark roast. Coffee's good here.

Shelburne Falls: I look for a seat. A woman laptops at the three-person table with her notebooks and a bag spread across the whole thing. There is a sweater draped across the couch behind her. The second couch has a dude manspreading smack in the middle of it. So I take the remaining option: a lumpy armchair. After awhile, the woman gets up to leave. It turns out the sweater is hers, and she's here with the guy on the couch. These *two* human beings took up a grand total of *nine seats*. Their ability to dominate a space — their overall obliviousness — fascinates me. Their complete disregard for others is almost impressive. I wonder what they think of themselves. Do they not even *suspect* they're assholes?

BWAH-OOOH
(DUNKIN DONUTS, EASTHAMPTON)

Bad pop country music dominates this space. Every cliché is proud and defiant, pushed through the overhead speakers at my head. I'm open-minded about many genres of music, but this hell-yeah-I'm-a-redneck, ain't-we-lucky, remember-when, back-porch, sippin'-beers, pickup trucks, ladies-as-objects garbage is a nightmare white dude shitfest created in a song-building laboratory, formulated and demographically targeted to be consumed by morons. "Our life is simple and hard and we *like* it that way!" Over-produced tepid rock with twangy vocals and an occasional lap steel *bwah-oooh*. Other than that, I am a benevolent and open-minded listener. My coffee and bagel are flavorless and the fluorescent lights make my eyes want to curl up and die and there are logos everywhere and now the drive-thru kid is singing along with the fucking radio oh god ain't we lucky.

HUMAN REMAINS
(DOUBLE D'S DINER, HATFIELD)

I walk into the Double D and I'm struck by how diner-y it is inside, which is a pleasant surprise since the exterior is a converted residential house. I walk in during a lull in room chatter, and I hear someone talking about pulling human remains out of the sea. I find this to be somewhat grisly and confusing, and it takes me a second to realize it's a CNN anchor on the TV and not a customer.

I sit at the counter and order. I add sugar to my coffee

and taste it. I add more, then some half and half. I taste it again. Hmmm, close, close. All I need now is coffee. There's a bottle on the counter labelled "Original Syrup." The dry erase board says "Happy 2015! Specials" and is otherwise blank. The standard collection of reproduction 'old-timey diner' tin signs hang behind the 1990's-era counter, which I suppose qualifies as old-timey to a certain subset of our population.

The eggs are good, and there's more ham on my plate than I eat in a week. A couple come in and sit down next to me. They order and proceed to sit in silence, hands folded and arms crossed. You'd think a person might not be able to read a diner placemat for long, but these two dig deep and really give it the ol' thrice-over. Self-storage, garage door installation, vinyl siding, small engine repair. By the time their food arrives, they must have it memorized.

One waitress helps the other waitress deliver food to a couple at a booth. "She gets the hash," she's told. Sounds like an old Soul Coughing song. The silent couple leaves, the husband taking great lengths to wish the busy waitress a good day, to draw her attention to the cash he's left under his wife's water glass. I fill my pockets with excess ham and pay my bill, going to great lengths to wish the busy waitress a good day, to draw her attention to the cash I've left under the ham I couldn't fit in my pockets.

Woodstar Cafe: A worker announces a customer's order is ready, pronouncing the name written on the order slip — "Zach" — as "Zatch." Which is kind of adorable when you stop and think about it.

THAT'S ALL, FOLKS
(AMHERST CINEMA, AMHERST)

I'm sitting in a dark theater thirty minutes before a Looney Tunes mini-marathon. It's chilly, but I have a cup of coffee to warm my bones. I'm sitting here because there was a too-stupid amount of time between ticket purchasing and showtime. When I'd decided to go to this event, it honestly hadn't occurred to me that I'd be drowned in a sea of children, because I have occasional bouts of total, absolute ignorance. Cartoons are for children, Tom.

Thankfully, as the theater fills, a young couple enter with no kids. Two old guys walk in, too. Age-diverse, non-parent humans. Good, good. It helps me feel less weird. The two old guys talk about *Chuck Amuck*, a book by Chuck Jones. It's solid and I recommend it. A slideshow of local ads plays on the screen. As a graphic designer, I'm critical of these things, but I'm determined to not delve into negative graphic designer griping. Nobody wants to read that. Hell, *I* don't want to read that. Words flash across the screen, written in a font whose name cannot be spoken. I breathe deeply.

Soon, the theater is filled with precociousness and excitement and giggles. Little feet kicking the back of my seat. Popcorn and chatter and anticipation. Moms narrate the ads, adding helpful, educational commentary. Two impossibly fashionable 7-year-olds sit down next to me. Jesus, are they on a *date?* The lights go down. I descend into the dark abyss with three school buses' worth of toddlers. Easy, Tommo. Eeeeaaaaasy. Everybody just take a potty break and *chill*.

It turns out watching Warner Bros. cartoons with a

theater full of kids is cute as hell, it really is. I realize this is the first time in my life I've watched cartoons as part of a crowd. Up til this afternoon, cartoon-watching had been a solitary entertainment from my mostly-solitary childhood. It's adorable to hear a little girl shout out "KITTY CAT!" as Mark Anthony pretends his new friend is a wind-up toy. The kids giggle as the lesson of mutually assured destruction from Duck Dodgers is completely lost on them. The children squeal in delight as Daffy Duck gets his face repeatedly blown off by a shotgun. I do, too. That motherfucker deserves it every goddamned time.

Esselon: A guy in a black trenchcoat throws his bag on the big communal table. He moves too fast and mumbles to himself, two qualities I look for when establishing a new tablemate relationship. He stabs at his salad like he's trying to keep tempo with the Queen song on the stereo. He pushes greens down his throat at an alarming rate. Trenchy bolts from his chair, looking for something near the cash register. A pen? Wifi password? Invisible government agent cat? Then he's back in his chair, mumbling again. I feel such a state of calm. This must be what it's like to hold space with a Buddhist monk. A manager sits at the table to do paperwork. He sings along with "Bohemian Rhapsody," high phonetic sounds, because he doesn't know any of the words. Man, I'm getting so much work done it's crazy.

SO HOT RIGHT NOW
(VESSEL / THE ELBOW ROOM, NORTHAMPTON)

Vessel (and its predecessor, The Elbow Room) was best-known as the smallest coffee shop in Northampton (or Massachusetts, or the planet), It was built into a space intended for an ATM, and there wasn't room in the tiny storefront for more than two customers at a time. This space constraint created an implied *exclusivity*, like a hot nightclub, or a secret house party, or Ebola. But now the funky space is even *harder* to get into, because several years ago, they cleverly locked the door and no longer exist as a business at *all*. That's right! This trendy cafe now holds ZERO CUSTOMERS AT A TIME. Talk about creating a BUZZ! I've been standing outside for HOURS! **I SIMPLY MUST. GET. IN.**

THE WHOLE SHEBANG
(THE STARBUCKS INSIDE STOP & SHOP, NORTHAMPTON)

Because of course there needs to be a Starbucks inside a Stop & Shop. Someone did business-y studies and came to business-y conclusions, and now this is a thing I can sit in. I order a coffee and enter the Starbucks Corner Area: a few tables, dark colored walls, wood paneling, and a row of brown floor tiles delineating where the cafe ends and the bakery department begins. It's as if someone has built a movie set in the corner of a supermarket.

I claim a table with my groceries and my cup of coffee and my seven-foot-long checkout receipt. On the back of the receipt, I'm presented with a coupon-looking

Kleenex coupon which is not a Kleenex coupon at all. It informs me that the *next* time I purchase Kleenex, I will receive a coupon redeemable on the *following* purchase. It is essentially a pre-coupon non-coupon announcing a possible upcoming coupon. This is why America is collapsing like a dying star. At a nearby table, a ponytailed man leans back in his chair, one hand in his jacket pocket, eyeing the comings and goings of the produce department with the cool grandiosity of an emperor surveying his court. A prerecorded voice informs us the deli department has rotisserie chickens fresh out of the oven. Then it informs us again.

Sitting in a chilly, too-dark corner of an otherwise chilly, too-bright cinderblock box isn't so bad. People avoid looking in this direction. I might as well be behind a two-way mirror, free to people-watch without fear of eye contact or retribution. "Why in God's name is that tall man writing in a notebook in a Starbucks in a supermarket on a Thursday afternoon?" a mother of two buying strawberries might ask, if my existence was at all acknowledged. "And is he writing about me?" The answers would be "Too much unsupervised free time" and "Yes."

There's something about the artifice and out-of-placeness of this cafe-themed corner that makes me think the whole shebang* will rotate into the wall on hidden tracks, and the Starbucks will be replaced by an innocent-looking bakery display. Like something from a *Get Smart* or *Scooby Doo* episode, a hidden-door-to-a-top-secret-lab type of thing.

There are people drinking Starbucks coffee while

---

*   Is the word "shebang" sexist? It sounds filthy.

grocery shopping. I think that's weird. I'm about to launch into a Classic Tom full-of-shit anti-consumerism diatribe when I'm suddenly distracted by a pie display. I love supermarket pie! Supermarket pie is like a bigger, softer version of convenience store pie, which I also love. Damn, now I'm absolutely going to buy a supermarket pie. It doesn't matter what kind of pie my supermarket pie is. I'm sorry but I won't share my supermarket pie with you. I'm not writing anymore. I need to buy this garbage thing.

The Haymarket: A mother and her teenaged son wait for their order. She steps away and I'm pretty sure the kid throws up a little. Like, he kind of steps forward awkwardly and looks down and then there's something wet near his feet. Mother returns, they confer, and she sends him out to the fire escape. She speaks with a barista, I assume pointing out the little puddle of watery cat food-looking stuff on the floor at the top of the stairs. You'd think "Problem Solved," but it's been almost ten minutes now, as employees shuttle food and dishes up and down the stairs, and I think it's been forgotten. No one seems to want to lasso this puke pony. I feel so fortunate to be here for this. I'm so so glad I can share this magical moment with you. Maybe I'm wrong, maybe it's soup. "Sure, yes, perhaps the young lad spilled some soup," the author convinces himself, unconvinced. "Some soup he was hiding in his esophagus." I move to a table across the room.

A MAN WHO KNOWS HOW TO
DINER (BLUEBONNET DINER, NORTHAMPTON)

I roll into the Bluebonnet Diner parking lot, blocked by a full-size double cab extended-whatever-the-fuck pickup truck. No way would this vehicle ever fit into a standard-sized parking space, so the driver has parked his emblem of masculine consumerism in the aisle of the parking lot. Ah, my fellow man.

I enter the Bluebonnet, deftly avoiding a head-whack on the low doorway, a reflex I've developed over years of whacking my head on low doorways. This is a Worcester Diner Car. I know this because it's written on the face of the clock over the counter. I sit. My waitress brings me a coffee without me asking. Her name is Jannine, which is a fantastic waitress name. Really top-notch.

A guy grabs the seat to my left, wrapping his coat around his counter stool and tying the sleeves together in a knot. Here is a man who knows how to diner like an expert. My coat is flopped over my stool, sleeves dragging all over the place. The guy to my right slouches over his iPhone and asks Siri about "A Hard Day's Night." She lets the whole diner know what she thinks of it. He mumbles something else into his phone. "FEBRUARY TWENTY-FIRST, NINETEEN SIXTY FIVE!" she bellows serenely. So, goddamnit, of course I'm going to Google it to see what the hell this guy is looking up, and the answer appears to be the assassination of Malcolm X. See, that guy's learning, and now I'm learning, and maybe you're learning, too. Eavesdropping Is Educational™ (cue the NBC "The More You Know" graphic).

Woodstar Cafe: A guy with stupid sunglasses orders a coffee. He's walking out the door when the cashier hollers him down, waving fifteen or so dollars in change he'd absentmindedly walked away from. He is embarrassed and grateful and apologetic, all of those things you emote in that situation. Then he walks away, no tip.

HAVE A TREMENDOUS DAY
(THE BLACK SHEEP, AMHERST)

I walk into a packed room, a Saturday afternoon crowd listens to a turban-wearing dude playing jazz guitar, accompanied by a non-turbaned dude on keyboard. When the song ends, no one claps. I drop my coat on a table and order a coffee to go. I always order my coffee to go. I'm a slow drinker.

"Have a tremendous day," the woman at the cash register says, handing me an empty cup. There's a weird vibe to it, I swear, it's not just me. As if she sees my laptop bag and my small purchase and is telling me to fuck off and die in a shallow grave in the woods alone. You go whipping out a word like "tremendous," and the odds are high you're employing sarcasm, employing it so well you're going to owe it a 1099 at the end of the year. In reaction to this perceived attitude, I throw money in the tip jar, because you're supposed to tip. Then I pour my own coffee, because it's self-serve coffee. So I just anxiety-tipped a person who did nothing and likely had no ill intentions. This is a thing I do. This is my life.

Four college-aged ladies sit at a table to my left, discussing the concept of working in exchange for money. The tone of the conversation is fresh and full of wonder. They've never delved into the topic. The conversation expands, covering things like *Lord Of The Rings* and polyamory and how annoying big scarves are. There's a loud ticking sound coming from the kitchen area, identical to the electric starter on my gas stove, which causes me actual discomfort, as if everything around me is about to explode in a ball of blue-tinged flame. This place has a relaxing atmosphere, aside from the imminent fear of horrific fire-death.

An Amherst College student sits to my right, reading Charles Darwin, studying her book with utmost seriousness. She eats an apple she keeps hidden on her lap. The girl sitting next to her has a bottle of Trader Joe's sparkling water on her table. Not a lot of local business supporters in attendance today, I guess. A mass murderer/child molester sits in silence at a table across the room. I say this with absolute certainty, based on his little mustache and suspicious '80s style metal-framed eyeglasses. I consider taking justice into my own hands: Eliminate this creepy dude and spare future victims a grisly fate. On the other hand, at least he ordered a sandwich.

SACK STABBER (ESSELON, HADLEY)

I powerslide into the Esselon parking lot doing about 45 mph sideways, because this stretch of Route 9 is an unforgiving hyper-luge that does not allow for slowing down or turning. I squeeze my Ford Focus into one of the too-small-for-a-Ford-Focus parking spaces.

This is a real nice place, with a lovely tin ceiling inside and a lovely garden seating area outside. There's also a weird porch in the middle. It's sort of inside and sort of out, enclosed in an ugly semi-permanent tent thing that makes the place drafty in the cold months and not cool enough during the hot ones. Burlap sacks of coffee beans separate the dining area from the ordering area. I am filled with a strong desire to bayonet them. I like the common table here because it's gigantic. I could push my laptop five feet in any direction and still not intrude on a tablemate's space. The chairs, on the other hand, are horrible. I don't even know how to describe them. They're wicker chairs, but made out of plastic. I guess I just described them? They're horrible.

Esselon is a bit expensive for my tastes. Dude, they have a ten dollar egg sandwich. Dude! Egg sandwiches are meant to exist as a cheap alternative to a full breakfast. A full breakfast here must cost upward of four thousand dollars (I'm estimating). Old white folks love this place, because old white folks love overpriced brunches. I come here for coffee and baked goods. Occasionally I'll have a sandwich from the glass case, a sandwich on the hardest roll you will ever encounter. It will peel your gums back and shave the veneer off your teeth, but overall: pretty tasty.

A few years back, I saw John Hodgman here, writing on his laptop. My communal table mates were giggling and whispering about the Mac/PC ads and giving each other nudges and annoying me. I would've said hello to him, but he was busy writing, and I see no good reason to interrupt a person when they're writing. These are the kind of famous person non-encounters I tend to have. My celebrity anecdotes are of the "I didn't talk to George Porter in a New Orleans bowling alley" or "I thought that guy was a shoplifter but I guess it's Peter Buck" variety. Anyway, the Hodgman sighting was back before I realized he's around the area quite often, about as common a western Massachusetts sight as Frank Black in tight bicycle pants, or Rachel Maddow buying kale chips at the co-op, or J Mascis seeming lost in a crosswalk.

> The Roost: Sitting next to a student. Her Chuck Taylors have flowers drawn on the toes, but it only appears that way. The drawings aren't ballpoint penned or Sharpied on, they are factory-applied defacement straight from Converse: a mass-produced, pre-approved expression of individuality. I plummet into a bottomless depression.

DONUT LUBE (ADAMS DONUT, GREENFIELD)

I drive up 91 and make it to Adams Donuts while they still have donuts. This is a momentous occasion for me. It's about a half hour drive for me, and I have historically arrived too late in the morning, when they've sold out of donuts for the day. I order a jelly stick and a sugar thing and a coffee. They are all damn fine.

The circular counter is full of old townies and I don't want to intrude upon that, so I sit in the corner and eavesdrop, as is my wont. Old dudes complain about dry waffles, bemoan the death of the newspaper industry, and retell jokes they heard on the radio. There is a conversation about grade school — nuns hitting kids with rulers, bus drivers throwing kids off buses and fistfighting them on the side of the road. You know, the good old days. In a politeness showdown, two older ladies disagree about who should get into line first. One guy insists Adams Donuts should be the setting of a sitcom. "Someone should call

Jerry Seinfeld!" he says. "There'd be tour buses coming by all the time, like *Cheers!*" He is genuinely excited about this idea.

Where did my donuts go? Whoops. They got et. I order two more: apple cider and jelly. I'm glad I didn't put any sugar in my coffee, because I'm inserting plenty into my mouth via fried dough. The jelly donut is the freshest donut I've had in a long time. I think maybe this coffee isn't so great after all, the more I drink it and the cooler it gets. But it's all right. It's donut lube, nothing more. It has a job to do and it does it. Can you say the same?

AN ADULT ALTERNATIVE
(DAM CAFE, HOLYOKE)

An old renovated brick building populated with inoffensive black furniture. Dark painted trim and mass-produced art prints inviting you to share a random moment with a cappuccino. Quaint, low-watt clear glass incandescent bulbs illuminate enlarged historic photos. The Dam Cafe is an independent business, but it gives every indication of being part of a corporate chain. There's barely any human touch here. Most of the decor has been ordered from the "cafe" section of a restaurant supply catalog. It's not that I'm offended by a small business aspiring to be a Starbucks, it's just that I don't understand the point, aside from making money, which is why I'd be a terrible small business owner, so more power to 'em.

I order a coffee and a sandwich and take a seat. My first sip of coffee is less-than-good. My mouth acclimates and what follows is tolerable. Four women sit at a nearby table, speaking Spanish, which complicates my attempts at eavesdropping and transcribing. It's along the lines of "¡Los [string of syllables] mira [string of syllables] hahahaha!" Two older ladies sit next to me, eating salads and gossiping about someone named Ginny while the satellite radio plays Adult Alternative music: A Counting Fucking Crows song from 2014. Who and where are these adults and what are they being provided an alternative to? Bring these people to me, and I will take this ballpoint pen and I will gut them like fish.

A sign mounted over the counter, written in the Papyrus font, suggests I sit long, talk much, and laugh often.

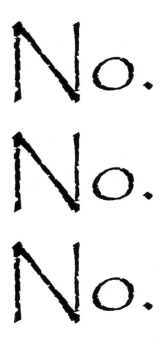

Small Oven: Behind the counter, a worker pounds a block of butter with a rolling pin. I'm talkin' wind-up-and-destroy. He's really beating the ever-loving shit out of it. It must be a supremely satisfying activity. I sit in the front window and soak in the view. Nails 2000n Spa is across the street, sporting that same Duran Duran-looking window graphic that every other nail salon on the planet has. Is that seriously the name of that place? Why is that little "n" there? The fuck?

POTPOURRI & DIESEL
(WHATELY DINER, WHATELY)

Named after Grammy Award-winning singer Jody Whately, and sporting a decidedly Weezer-by-way-of-Van-Halen logo on its menus, the Whately Diner is part of a legit truck stop. The diner is a fantastic building on the crumbling edge of a vast expanse of asphalt, surrounded by the grumble of idling big rigs. The parking lot smells like potpourri and diesel fuel, due to the Yankee Candle headquarters down the street, which manufactures potpourri and diesel fuel-scented candles.

A roadtripping couple step out of their Toyota and stretch, each cradling an armload of empty Dunkin Donuts cups and energy drink bottles, destined for the parking lot trash barrel. The woman walks in and asks a waitress if she can use the restroom. "You don't have to ask," the waitress says. "We're a truck stop." I order a western omelet and hash browns and a coffee. They are terrible. I endure them silently. The smiling waitress is cute and practices good eye contact, which must help with tips immensely. She asks me if I'd like anything else, and I politely say "No, thank you" instead of "DEAR GOD NO PLEASE NO." Meanwhile, the notification light on my phone keeps trying to notify me of shit. Little blinky green motherfucker. I've turned off so many notifications, but there are always more. I flip my phone face-down on the table. The notification light burns a hole through the tabletop and shines its insistent asshole green light on my foot.

NOT STARBUCKS!
(BARNES & NOBLE, HADLEY)

I walk into Barnes & Noble on a Sunday afternoon, past the magazine section, and into the Barnes & Noble Cafe, which serves Starbucks coffee. Let me be clear: This is not a Starbucks. The menu board bears the Starbucks logo, as do the cups and cup sleeves and table tents, but this is *not* a Starbucks location. Do you understand me? Do *not* refer to this half-walled-off area as Starbucks. If you do, sweatervested employees will swoop in and beat you with unsold issues of *GQ*.

Good ol' Barnes & Noble, the new American library. Several students are laptopping, their tables stacked high with (FREE!) books as they work on papers. I wait in line behind two whispering women, which of course forces me to listen more intently. From what I can discern, they're discussing wildly unsecretive things: laundry, gas stations, candy. I'd love to weave these elements into a narrative worth whispering about. Ooooh! Writing challenge!

I order a coffee and a biscotto. I sit up straight and push my shoulders back, daring someone to challenge my word usage, but no one notices, because I'm writing. The coffee is weak, the Italian cookie is hard and dry. I sit in an area decorated with gigantic reproductions of classic book art: *A Tree Grows In Brooklyn* (Smith), *Death Of A Salesman* (Miller), *For Whom The Bell Tolls* (Metallica). There's a huge Ayn Rand book cover which compels a minimum of one liberally-minded person per day to sigh and roll their eyes, publicly signifying their disapproval of her, her work, and her fans. A declaration of non-affiliation. This is a behavior some people are compelled to exhibit.

The Not-Starbucks fills up as the afternoon progresses. There's an old man reading news on his gigantic, loud laptop. There's a woman with purple hair who doesn't seem like the type of person to have purple hair. As I prepare to abandon the two-foot-tall pile of magazines on my table, a couple of UMASS girls sitting behind me debrief over a first date. One of them met a boy at a laundromat. They went to a gas station for some candy, and then they murdered a hobo with a tire iron. Jeez, ladies! Keep your voices down!

ON THE CUSP OF RETRO-UGLY
(SUNRISE OVER FLORENCE CAFE, FLORENCE)

The radio is not-quite-tuned to a classic rock station. Journey, a rock-n-roll fantasy, "Sweet Child O' Mine." I didn't realize this place existed until a couple of weeks ago. At first, I thought it was a reincarnation of Sunraise, an Easthampton bakery that closed a few years ago, but I had misread their sign, which is ripe for misreading.

The coffee is good. So is the big cookie I ordered. The sandwich menu looks promising, but I don't want a sandwich, so I don't order one. The room itself is from my aesthetic nightmares: commercial carpeting, white metal tube chairs circa 1981, drop ceiling, and booths on the cusp of being retro-ugly, but today they're just regular-ugly. One wall is lined with big windows, but the curtains are drawn shut. The overhead fluorescent lights are on instead, because naturally, a place named Sunrise Over Florence wouldn't want to expose its customers to sunlight or Florence.

"This made the whole trip worth it," a woman says to her friends as she walks away from the register. She shows them her change. "An Everglades quarter." She has collected all of the state quarters, she tells them. They're doing national parks now. I would mock her, except I sort of collect vintage soda bottles, so who the hell am I to talk? Also, I'm trying to be less of an asshole. Enjoy your fucking quarters, lady. Enjoy the shit out of them.

I use the restroom on my way out. There are four spare chairs facing the toilet, which I find unnerving. What goes on in here? "Tiny Dancer" fades further into static.

STUNG BY MANY BEES
(RAO'S, NORTHAMPTON)

As I turn to walk through the front entrance of Thornes Marketplace, I'm almost sideswiped by a man desperate to avoid eye contact with a homeless guy. We enter the creaky-floored palace of commerce together, trapped behind a slow-moving young man who appears to be enthralled with early 20th-century fashion, but not the ironing or grooming that originally accompanied it. After a quick stop at Acme Surplus for some no-brand packing tape, I stop by the Rao's counter and order a small coffee. Their small is a particularly small small, priced on par with everyone else's regular small. Or maybe it's an optical illusion. Maybe my hands are gigantic and swollen and I should get to the emergency room because I have been stung by many bees. Whatever the reason, I find myself holding a very small cup.

The seating area here is two loose clusters of tables flanking Thornes' main shopping thoroughfare. During busy times, it must be wall-to-wall ass-viewing here, which in some worlds might be a positive thing, but who are we kidding, not here. I choose a table tucked in a corner, so as to not be out in the middle of everything. A woman compliments her friend on shopping locally. A little girl shows her mother how to use her own iPad. The floors of the old building never stop creaking. "SHIMS EXIST!" I shout, but no one hears me, because of the creaking.

THIRTY-SEVEN MINUTES
(THE YELLOW SOFA, NORTHAMPTON)

3:55 — A loud annoying man fills out a job application. HE REALLY LOVES THE VIBE HERE. He orders an iced coffee. MMM THIS IS SO GOOD. I've never heard a person broadcast such obnoxious, room-filling, straw-sucking sounds. I think he finished the drink and now he's just trying to terrorize the ice. I hope he gets the job. I'd love to see him again.

4:01 — I'm going to assume this loud annoying man is under the influence of a narcotic which makes him twitchy and unbearable. He sucks on his goddamned straw the whole walk to the trashcan. He orders another drink.

4:06 — The loud annoying man won't stop talking to the girl trapped at the register. Everyone in the room learns he's gay, where he's lived, his current job, his past jobs, where he went to school, and where his mom lives. He loves Go-Berry, and he wants to go to Diva's. He wants to know who to talk to about the job. He wants to know more about open-mic night. Everyone here now knows this man's phone number and that it takes him a really, really long time to fill out a one-page job application. He's curious who the baker is. Do they serve beer here? His phone rings. His ringtone is a voice saying his name. His crotch calls out his name.

4:12 — The loud annoying man goes to the bathroom. The room falls into a delicate and precious silence. We all take deep breaths and feel a sense of peacefu—

4:15 — Jesusfuckingchrist the loud annoying man is singing now. His boyfriend is here, too, by the way. They're both applying for the same job. I haven't mentioned him until now because he's so quiet. They must have amazing arguments with each other. Like Kim Kelly and Daniel Desario in the Weir's kitchen.

4:21 — The loud annoying man and his boyfriend manage to drop the cream dispenser twice (once each) and knock over a chair. They're going to be at Diva's tonight if anybody wants to meet up. He's not sure how much the cover is, but he isn't worried.

4:32 — The loud annoying man examines a jar of tea leaves. "They all smell so good," he says reverently. "The world is just such an amazing place." His boyfriend warns him to be careful. "I'm not going to drop them, I just want to smell them." He turns to another customer. "Do you come here a lot?" They stride out. I think it was performance art. Pretty well-choreographed. The world is just such an amazing place.

> "Tripping is like a reset button."
> "Yeah."
> "I do it around twice a year. I'm a better person for it."
> "Same. Same."
> *– Two self-described 'weirdo art freaks,'*
> *Shelburne Falls Coffee Roasters*

COFFEE SHED
(DUSTY ROSE'S CREAMERY, HADLEY)

If you're ever driving through Hadley, Massachusetts and you want a cup of coffee, yet you've chosen to bypass Esselon, Donut Man and Dunkin Donuts, and you just can't wait another two minutes to reach another Dunkin Donuts, or Starbucks, or Panera, or Shelburne Falls Coffee Roasters, or Stables, then I recommend you stop by Dusty Rose's Creamery.

I don't know who Dusty Rose is, but I believe her to be a woman with a clear aesthetic vision, transforming this small storage shed-sized building into a drive-thru snack stop that still looks exactly like a small storage shed. The seating area, mere feet from an aggressive stretch of Route 9, is a strange showcase of different garden and yard furniture. Pink wooden deck chairs, wrought iron chairs, a wooden swing for two. A patio of flagstone, a walkway of brick, a different walkway of cement pavers. Two different types of gravel under two different styles of picnic tables. A plastic veranda and an adorable miniature bench. Flower boxes and a birdbath and randomly placed rock walls complete this odd outdoor display. I don't think I've ever seen anyone sitting out here before.

I sit at a picnic table, no shade in sight, alone with my coffee and a bagel. All I hear is tires on asphalt. This whole stretch of road is depressing as hell, it really is. I try to sit for awhile, honest, but I surrender pretty fast. I get in my car and head for Home Depot, where I'm going to see all of this garden furniture again, arranged the same exact way. Thank Christ I'm turning right. I wouldn't turn left onto this road for a hundred dollars.

Roost: A young woman strides in and sits at the counter. I fall in love with her because of her bangs. Black, cut in a crisp line. Some ladies can carry a whole look with good hair. I'll probably forget everything about her by the time I get home, but I'll remember those bangs. Well, and her jacket. She has a cool jacket, too.

> "There are plenty of places to sit. It's always fun to try new things."
> *— Mother to her children, Big Y Cafe*

A JAZZ DISAGREEMENT
(NORTHAMPTON COFFEE, NORTHAMPTON)

Sitting at a window seat at Northampton Coffee. On the stereo, a terrible saxophone argues with a terrible piano in an unappetizing jazz disagreement, as the barista takes excessive pride in his ability to form words and push them out of his mouth. He tells his coworker that generic medications at Stop & Shop are the same as the brand name ones, but cheaper. "The silver snake slid down the slippery slide sideways," he says to a customer. He describes someone's hair as being "like Ronald McDonald from the 80s, or my mom's perm." He talks about how many Dodge Chargers were used in *The Dukes Of Hazzard*. He is a fountain of pointless bullshit, a relentless spurt of full-volume trivia.

A steady stream of attractive people park, come in, order coffees and leave. Golfs and Yarises and RAV4s — a rainbow of different grays and dark whites and light black vehicles — fill and vacate the parking spaces along Pleasant Street. A woman pulls up in her Forester, finishes the coffee in her travel mug, and comes in for more. No one throws a single dime into the meters, either. That's some carpe diem shit, right there. I can't do it, I just can't.

I overhear a story about a touring musician, but I miss overhearing his name. For the sake of retelling, let's pretend it was Rick Springfield: Rick Springfield is in town for a show, and he goes to Turn It Up. He finds a treasure trove of his own rarities and collectibles, out-of-print stuff he no longer has personal copies of. Embarrassed, he walks up to the counter with a big pile of his own CDs. After ringing up the first three or four discs, the cashier comments "You must really like this guy." Rick Springfield is mortified, unable to admit that he is Rick Springfield. He leaves quietly with his treasures.

BANGBANGBANGBANG

A woman is trapped in the bathroom due to a faulty doorknob. She pounds hard on the door to be heard above the din of the cafe. Everyone laughs about it once she's out, for some reason. Ha-ha. "She was trapped in the bathroom," one customer informs another. People share stories of being trapped in and/or locked out of various bathrooms. This is how humans relate to each other.

A Smithie runs her laptop power cord across an area where people walk, behind my chair, across another area where people walk, to a distant wall outlet. She turns to her friends and laughs. "This is *such* a hazard!" No one condemns or even comments on her unacceptable behavior. What the fuck is wrong with her, me, us, everybody.

Woodstar Cafe: There are thirteen tables in the main seating area. I am sitting at one of them, and the other twelve are empty. A man walks in, orders, and sits next to me. He is now on my terrorist watch list.

MAYBE I'M ALREADY DEAD
(DUNKIN DONUTS, MAIN ST, NORTHAMPTON)

I walk past two of my favorite coffee places (plus about seven other perfectly fine options) and visit the Dunkin Donuts on Main Street. It's been here for a decade or something, but this is my first visit. I wear my Red Sox hat so I blend in with the natives — New England camouflage. I order an iced coffee (one cream, one sugar) and sit at a table bolted to the floor. My drink is delicious candy, and I drink it too fast.

Bags are piled on the window seats. The bag owners stand out on the sidewalk, smoking cigarettes and liberating Red Bull cans from a city trash barrel. The front window offers a perfectly-framed view of the Academy Of Music, one of the most beautiful buildings in the region. Next door to this Dunkin is Filo's Greek Taverna, a storefront featuring one of the great design atrocities of the last century. I can't stress enough how shitty the Filo's sign is. I want to smash into it with a truck, but I'm not sure anyone would notice the difference. Maybe a truck already *has* smashed into it, I don't know. I'm just grateful I can't see it from here.

A woman in a Red Sox jacket concentrates on a word puzzle book on a clipboard. The ceiling speakers emit jazz while a small boombox behind the counter plays classic rock. "Brown Eyed Girl" and "Separate Ways" and "Tonight, Tonight" compete with saxophones and pianos and more fucking saxophones. This, to me, is a maddening, intolerable mess of conflicting rhythms and keys. A kid at another table cranks up his headphones, so the trebly beat of his hip-hop bleeds into the mix. I'm going to die. Maybe I'm already dead.

This Dunkin location serves cancer-voiced men and pajama bottom-wearing women who call everyone "honey." Construction dudes and lazy-eyed kitchen workers. An elderly woman with an ankle brace hobbles in with her walker and a Stuart Hall paperback. A couple erupts in a shouting argument.

Outside, a PVTA bus kneels at the curb. A Funky Cab waits at the light next to a Toyota Matrix with no hubcaps (they never have hubcaps). A Hodge City Mechanical truck edges around the bus. Have you ever seen one of these trucks? On the passenger door, there's a crude drawing of Scooby-Doo's head coming out of the top of a closed toilet. I've never met anyone who knows why it's there, or what it means, or where the fuck "Hodge City" is. "High five! Go Tampa! Go Tampa!" the Dunkin worker shouts at a customer. They high five. "No Vancouvah! No offense, but I don't want Chicago to win." Where am I? Where is this place? The bus windows reflects the Filo's sign. I shudder.

WHAT MOOD YOU MIGHT CATCH ME IN (STARBUCKS, AMHERST)

I stop into Rao's on a Saturday morning, but it's packed: two hundred people using five hundred wifi-enabled devices. I wander towards the main intersection, sharing the sidewalk with young men with questionably-trimmed facial hair and brightly-colored Ray-Bans and shirts without sleeves. I end up at Starbucks, because that's what Starbucks is for. You end up there. I get a table next to a wall outlet, which I figured would be coveted by laptoppers, but then I notice wall outlets everywhere. Good ol' corporate electricity, man.

Starbucks has reusable plastic cups designed to look like to-go iced coffee cups. I find this to be amusing or clever or sad, depending on what mood you might catch me in. There are gigantic photos on the wall, close-up photos of coffee bean mounds and grinders and shit. The beans are bigger than my thumb. A happy pop song shuffles out of the speakers in the ceiling. I can picture the barefoot white man who is responsible for it, his puka necklace against his tan skin. He just wants to LIVE LIFE, y'know? The song is programmed to include the precise doses of handclapping and ascending ukulele chords. It is bright and cheery. It is so strategically inoffensive, it induces rage. A Starbucks employee wheels a large, full garbage can through the main dining area and out the front door. Without moving my head, I count fifteen Starbucks logos and eight Apple logos within my field of vision.

I try and connect my phone to the free Google wifi, but my Google phone and my Google browser don't seem to like it (to be fair, this phone doesn't seem to like much).

I pack up my stuff. Two UMASS girls hover nearby and wait for me to vacate my table, but they're weird about it. They feel the need to pretend they're disinterested, as if they're pulling a fast one over on me. They turn away and communicate with exaggerated eye movements. "Get ready to swoop in!" one says with her eyeballs. "The old must be eradicated from the Earth," the other responds by flaring her nostrils. I drop into my electric mobility scooter adorned with American flags and reflective safety tape and roll out the front door with the garbage. Just take the fucking table, ladies.

FIFTY-EIGHT MUTUAL
FRIENDS (BRUEGGER'S BAGELS, NORTHAMPTON)

"No cinnamon raisin?" the woman in front of me repeats back to the bagel maker. She ponders this terrible situation for a moment, says "Thank you," and walks out.

I step up. "What can I get for you?" the bagel maker asks me. I'd wanted a cinnamon raisin bagel, too, god damn it! I order a sesame bagel and a coffee. Fucksticks.

I sit at the front window table and people-watch. A steady stream of annoyed, distracted people exit CVS, juggling change and giant receipts and prescriptions. The two illegal parking spaces in front of the store stay busy. A woman walks by with a Turn It Up! bag, and I'm reminded that I designed that logo, maybe sixteen or seventeen years ago now? A whole human being teenager ago. That's a getting-old thing, when you mark time in teenagers. I see a guy wearing a Hot Chocolate Run hat. Boom. Made it. New Century Theater banner on the courthouse fence. Mmm-hmmm. I've seen cars display two or three bumper stickers I've designed. It's an odd and good thing, to feel like you're part of a place.

I can see the Calvin Theater marquee from here. Damned thing got hit by a truck again. Is it too impossible to install two metal posts on the curb below? Could this simple solution not get worked out with the city somehow? I recognize every few passing faces, people who aren't quite acquaintances, even after twenty years of living here. If I knew their names, I could look them up on Facebook and discover we have fifty-eight mutual friends, and then we could continue to not know each other.

You know that loud downtown lady? The one who goes off her meds sometimes and shouts across the street at you and calls you a cocksucker? Her name's Tracy. She's at Bruegger's this morning, in a friendly, non-shouty state. The workers give her a free sandwich. She limps around, muttering but smiling. "My mother went through a divorce!" she barks. "Hey you wanna see a picture of Marilyn Monroe?" she asks no one. Tracy is like an Amy Sedaris character with all the humor stripped away.

Bruegger's. More sweatpants here, fewer skinny jeans. More working class, fewer college kids. Not many laptoppers, not a lot of ironic facial hair. A mix of Hamp and Noho. The bulletin board is at least ten flyers thick. My table is covered in sesame seeds. CVS receipts blow down the sidewalk. Heart of downtown.

Bliss Cafe: I order an iced coffee for here. The worker, seeming a little preoccupied, makes an iced coffee for here and hands it to a woman who was waiting before I came in. "This was to go," she corrects him. He apologizes, puts the iced coffee into a to go cup, and hands it to her. She leaves. *Aww, that was totally my coffee,* I think to myself. The worker starts making a blueberry smoothie. I watch and wait. I keep waiting. He's blending things. Examining bags of kale or something. He's focused. After civilizations have disappeared under the ever-shifting sands of time, I speak up and say that I'm still waiting for an iced coffee. He apologizes and makes one for me.

I sit and write, and a short while later he comes out with the blueberry smoothie. There is no customer waiting for a blueberry smoothie. There are no customers waiting for anything. Who ordered the blueberry smoothie? He discusses it with his co-workers, but they didn't notice. Did that woman order a blueberry smoothie and then accept my iced coffee instead? Did she forget what she ordered? Did her beverage choice not matter to her? Is there another person involved in this word problem? When did the train leave the station? I drink my coffee. It's good. A cloud of mystery hangs over the room. *Ghost order!*

> **"I need to step off the curb and tell him to cool his jets."**
> *– Man on phone, Dunkin Donuts*

INEVITABLY DECAPITATED
(THE HAYMARKET, NORTHAMPTON)

I have a long-running relationship with The Haymarket. This was my destination for marathon sitting and sketchbook scribbling and Smithie-pining in my early years in the Pioneer Valley. I'd rent a table for the price of a small cup of coffee and draw comics about non-superheroes who would inevitably get decapitated, only to replace their missing head with a nearby kitchen appliance or large spider.

How many times has this place been renovated? I remember the weird crawl space over the counter when it was a street-level cafe. I remember the room of books under the stairs when it became a two-story downtown juggernaut. There was a kitchen downstairs, and then it was a different kitchen with a counter. Now it's a restaurant downstairs, so I don't sit there anymore. The Haymarket is a cozy bunch of rooms covered in many layers of paint, filled with attractive people covered in many layers of tattoos. The coffee is always acceptable. The cookies are always good. I order one with banana and oatmeal and chocolate chips

and a bunch of other crap in it. It's great.

I spill coffee on my notebook, which is totally okay, because it cost a dollar at Acme Surplus. I've never quite understood people who buy nice journals. I assume that for them, the journal is the final product. That is not my worldview. I need scrap paper, a place for a messy first draft full of crossing out and arrows and margin notes. My illegible scrawls either get typed up or forgotten. A notebook is transient and ethereal to me, like a hobo on rollerblades.

I get up to use the bathroom and miss it by two seconds. Dude swoops in and gets there before me. Fine. I wait outside the door, bursting with patience and urine. Two people — TWO! — stride past me and try the door. TWO! Like, they didn't think I'd *checked?* Or they're choosing to ignore the tall guy four inches away from them who's *clearly* standing and waiting? What's wrong with these goddamned toilet vultures? STEP THE FUCK BACK I NEED TO WEE. And now I bet the guy's gonna come out of the bathroom and give me a dirty look for trying the doorknob over and over. You just can't win, you really can't.

WHAT FOODS THESE MORSELS BE! (DONUT DIP, WEST SPRINGFIELD)

There are no seats at Donut Dip, so I'm standing at the window counter, ballpointing a few brief sentences, fingers covered in sugar. I try to be mindful of my posture. I'm a semi-reformed sloucher, trying to stay upright with shoulders back, but I end up feeling like C-3PO. It's my lot in life. No music in here, only refrigerator hum and two young ladies behind the glass cases not talking to each other. The smallest iced coffee here is twice as big as a coffee pot. Great hand-painted signs behind the register, and my jelly donut is fine, damned fine. Across the four-lane road is a cemetery I've never noticed before and a Hooter's with a full parking lot. The Donut Dip bag says "What Foods These Morsels Be!" This is the finest slogan I have ever seen.

I feel rushed, scribbling a series of tweets, a telegram, a bullet-point list. It is within the realm of possibility that sugar and caffeine play a role in this feeling. I already ate my donuts, and I still have three gallons of coffee left. Should I get more donuts to go? How does a person do that? Doesn't everyone just eat them all in the car on the ride home? Why are my hands trembling?

Tandem Bagel: There are two tip jars here, allowing the customer to vote for one kind of meaningless thing or another. This is a common cafe shtick now, an attempt to turn tipping into a fun game. Cutesy signs, tapping into the consumer's inherent need to express an opinion on bullshit. I bet it's also a great way for business owners to better understand their customers' preferences and desires. Winter or fall? *Star Wars* or *Star Trek?* Oral or Anal? "We've had an enthusiastic customer response to anal," a manager reports at a staff meeting. "Let's split up into teams and brainstorm on some anal-themed pastries and desserts!" I get it, I really do. The tip-voting thing is a great idea. I think cafes should have three tip jars. Maybe four. Let's vote on it.

PIE. (FLORENCE PIE BAR, FLORENCE)

Pie bar. Two words, one syllable each, three letters each. Pie bar. Is there a more wonderful, perfectly-balanced combination of words to be had? So pure. So simple. So pie. So bar. I visit Florence Pie Bar on a Thursday afternoon, ordering a slice and a coffee from a city councilor. This is the sort of business that had its shit together right out of the gate. Like The Quarters in Hadley, these folks opened with a clear identity, a clear goal, and they've given people something they want in a room worth sitting in. My first visit to the pie bar and I want to buy a mug. That there is good business-makin'!

After my slice of apple lattice is gone, I snag one of the last slices of blueberry from Councilor At-Large Dwight.

Not the last for the day — though they usually run out of everything by the end of the day — but for the season. Two-pie lunch, man. There's nothing like a motherfucking two-pie lunch.

"Pie bar." Let the words roll around in your mouth. "Pie bar." Pie. Bar.

Pie bar!

GO GOOGLE OGLE

The free computer access area is bustling — lots of hubbub, potato chip bag sounds, unsilenced cell phones — so I take my Woodstar coffee to one of the big tables, the giant ones with built-in lights and electrical outlets. I'd love to have one of these suckers in my home, if only I had a spare basketball court to put one in. I forget if outside drinks are allowed in here, so I'm nervous, but I remember they used to have a coffee/snack bar in the lobby a couple years back, so they must, right? They must. A dude walks by with a gigantic Dunkin Donuts iced coffee. Okay, anxiety released.

I'm sitting in the reference section. How often do these puppies get cracked open nowadays? The 12-volume *New Catholic Encyclopedia*. The 20-volume *McGraw Hill Encyclopedia of Science and Technology*. Five volumes on Africana. Three books on world coins. There's a 22-volume *World Encyclopedia* with a single graphic image running across the spines, but the set is split onto two shelves, ruining the effect and offending the orderly part of my brain.

I don't take books out of the library much anymore. I can't stand having a time limit to read something, even though I know damn well I could renew. But I'm a slow and infrequent reader, and I don't want recreational deadlines in my life. My real problem is I buy books, and they sit on a shelf for three or four years before I get around to reading them. So I already have my own library, I guess. But I borrow DVDs here, discs donated from good ol' Pleasant Street Theater Video. A seven day loan for a movie is a *good* thing for me. It is manageable, and a good motivator to watch a film within a reasonable period of time.

I move to the upper level and grab a comfy-looking chair overlooking the checkout desks. There's another guy sitting in the other comfy chair ogling one of the young librarians below. But who am I to judge? I'm ogling, too, I guess. I'm ogling everybody. The difference is I'm writing about it, and I'm a little less creepy. *Ogling*. What a bizarre word. Where's a word like that come from? If only there was a place I could go to look up its derivation. I know, I'll check the internet.

"Three hundred and eighty-five seconds for that," a McDonald's worker tells her trainee, slamming the microwave door shut. The chatter behind the counter is constant, tense, confused. "Don't make that double order," I hear someone shout. "Corporate is watching us!" a manager warns. Two workers make a judgment call on what might be my breakfast: "Would you eat that egg?"

An old guy stands by the counter, waiting with his wife for their order. They get their food from a harried 18-year old. The man asks for syrup. There are five or eight people behind the counter, but he somehow doesn't get a response or syrup. He asks again. He asks nine more times. He can see the syrup packets behind the counter. "They're right there," he says, pointing.

THE LEAST I CAN DO
(FACES CAFE, NORTHAMPTON)

I stride past the kitten-themed sunglasses and the fart-scented soaps and the caffeinated gay peanut butter and the ukulele keychains and the zombie unicorn masks, making my way to the back of Faces' first floor. Until a month ago, it was full of greeting cards. Now it's not-full of cafe customers. I sit alone, outnumbered by fluorescent light banks. But "Bootylicious" is on, there's free wifi, and the coffee's okay. I pay eight dollars for a sandwich, because I'm already quite sure I'll never return after writing these paragraphs, so I figure it's the least I can do for the local economy. I pick a table in the corner while long-time Faces employee Mike patrols the toy section for shoplifters, or maybe he's just bored, I don't know. A bootylicious girl walks in and leans over the counter to talk to the cashier and the manager, who have nothing else to do. Is she a customer? No, another employee.

Now "Dancing Queen" is on the stereo. The bacon in my sandwich is so hard, I worry I've bitten into a toothpick. A young man wanders in with a group of friends. They giggle at the drink case like it's a hilarious display of wacky t-shirt designs. "I'm going back to the store part of the store," he says. An older man skirts the edge of the cafe area, confounded by the open expanse of floor dotted with metal chairs and metal tables and Tom Pappalardos. "Get Into The Groove" comes on the stereo. At this point, I'm only mentioning songs because there's not much else to observe. A lady with a puffy vest looks at a WICKED HUGE BRUINS FAN t-shirt. A girl looking at, Jesus, I don't know, dildos shaped like Sriracha bottles or something? *Angry Birds Star Wars* rub-on tattoos? What the fuck does this place sell? Anyway, she's perusing nearby products and giving me sidelong glances. Not a "Hey, handsome man" look. It's more of a "Oh, look at the sad panda at the zoo" type of look. A Faces employee restocks a t-shirt. As in, a single t-shirt. He takes his time. Billie Holiday sings a song. I can't hear her voice without thinking of David Sedaris.

A woman crosses the threshold! She approaches the counter! "Hello!" says the counter worker. "Hello!" says the manager. I'm tempted to welcome her, too. "Please! Come in! Sit with me! Let me buy you a toothpick sandwich!" She asks them where the stairway is and leaves when she gets her answer. But then a couple comes in and put their stuff on a table! Here we go! Finally! Customers! FIRE UP THE MICROWAVE, BOYS! IT'S ABOUT TO GET— Oh wait, they're just using the bathroom in the back corner of the store. "The Rainbow" by Ween comes on. It's the best part of this experience so far. Mike walks over and gets a cup of coffee. Am I in the Faces break room? Is that what's happening? Do I work here now? Should I restock a t-shirt?

"He used to visit me periodically, for about six years after he died."
– Woman discussing her father's ghost, The Haymarket

Shelburne Falls Coffee Roasters: A man walks in with a brand new toilet seat from Manchester Hardware. A woman laughs too-loudly as she reads a printout of an article about Donald Trump. I pick up my phone and skim Facebook, Instagram, email. Back to Facebook. I put my phone down and wonder what time it is. Maybe the reason I picked up the phone in the first place was to check the time? The clock was right there — in the corner of the screen I was looking at — the whole time. Jesus, it's like I'm carrying around a black hole in my pocket. I check Facebook.

ALREADY IN THE RED
(SILVER SPOON, EASTHAMPTON)

It's never pleasant starting a day with a headache. It seems unfair and cruel to wake up already in the red. I drive over to The Silver Spoon, squinting at the overcast sky.

I stumble to the counter and a merciful waitress hands me a cup of coffee. I order the Lumberjack breakfast— eggs, meats, homefries, and pancakes—even though the Lumberjill is a bit smaller and I'm not super-starved or anything. But there are gender norms and expectations to conform to, people! Boys drink Buck Rogers and girls drink Shirley Temples! *Everyone knows this!* So I will force Jack down my throat. Hmm, what?

This is the kind of place where I can't tell who my waitress is. One young lady brings the coffee, another takes my order, another delivers it, another offers a refill. It's not that I need to know, it's just that I like to know who to bother in case I need to bother someone, even though I hate bothering anyone.

Two old men sit facing each other in two adjacent booths. It's hard to say whether they're conversing or just bellowing declarative statements towards each other. On the topic of the Vietnam war, one guy says "I don't know about anyone else, but I had a good time over there!"

I watch the girl at the grill, slipping the spatula under some over-easy eggs and flipping with deft skill. No broke yolks here. Clean, professional, a practiced flip. When I flip an over-easy egg, it becomes a crime scene, with Detectives Bunk and McNulty shaking their heads in disgust and muttering "Fuck fuck fuck."

Damn, these homefries are great. I eat my Lumberjack, every bite. WHO'S A BIG BOY!

PICK AGAIN (DENNY'S, HOLYOKE)

I'm not sure if I've ever set foot in a Denny's restaurant during daylight hours, and if I have, it was twenty-plus years ago. It's a Tuesday afternoon and I've just bought a scratch-and-dent refrigerator at the Sears outlet (for the record, a dent is worth approximately -$230). The Denny's is in the same shopping plaza, an endless expanse of obliterated asphalt, so I figured why not.

I'm greeted by a claw machine full of stuffed animals by the entrance. More businesses need these. I order an Original Grand Slam and a coffee. My fork and spoon have crusty shit on them. The food arrives too quickly, the meat cool and the pancakes radiating heat like miniature suns. The sausages worry me and the fake maple syrup comforts me. When I finish my scrambled eggs, I remember I'd ordered over easy.

There's a Marvel/*Fantastic Four* promotion happening. I could've gotten a Thing Burger. The waitress clears the dishes from the next booth, saying "Let me steal these from you." She collects meal debris from a pale, goateed gamer who has left his apartment for the first time in days. Trust me on this one. My coffee mug lets me know "A good diner has open doors, open arms and open hearts," but apparently not Oxford commas.

"Grandma! Drink your soda!" a teenage boy in the next booth demands from his grandmother. "Oh, that's my soda. Ha ha!" She is diabetic, everyone in earshot learns. He reads the menu out loud to her, alternating personas: The Best Grandson Angel versus The Impatient Verbally Abusive Prick. "I can't decide, Grammy!" He asks her to pick a number between one and ten. Whatever number she picks is the wrong one. "Aww, you suck!" he says in a friendly tone that isn't friendly at all. "Now I have to order the Baja Quesadilla Burger!" He tells her to pick again, but she refuses. He gets mad, persistent, insistent, and she keeps refusing. "Pick again. Pick again." This goes on for a full two or three minutes, this boy-man demanding she re-pick a number. She relents and says "Ten." Whatever item number ten is, he doesn't approve, and orders Zesty Nachos instead.

> Northampton Coffee: A man stands up from one of the weird narrow tables bolted to the wall, knocking his water glass off the weird table's weird edge. He almost catches it — a fumbling but valiant attempt. Alas, the glass bounces off his fingertips. Then a less-helpful instinct takes over and HE KICKS THE GLASS IN MIDAIR LIKE IT'S A HACKY SACK.

TWO MORE CUPS OF COFFEE
(MANHAN CAFE & BLISS, EASTHAMPTON)

A trio of ladies play backgammon in the front window of Manhan Cafe. It's early afternoon, the day after an ice storm. My glasses fog up when I walk into the place, but there's no menu board to read and no one else to bump into, so I stand there wiping my lenses on my t-shirt while the owner observes from behind the register. Not even a hello. I keep my earflap hat on because my hair is a greasy mess. I ask the man if there are any bagels, since the counter display is empty. He reveals a cache of secret bagels hidden behind the counter in a Tupperware container. I order a plain bagel and a coffee. According to a sign taped to the table I sit at, it's reserved for three people or more. Should that be 'Three or more people'? Either way, I sit there. I've been attempting to visit Manhan Cafe for a few months now. Every time I walk by, they're either closed, about to close, or in the process of closing. After my first sip of coffee, I decide to never get coffee here again.

It's pretty quiet, except for the clatter of backgammon dice and an occasional car slushing down Cottage Street. A cheap Yamaha acoustic leans on a guitar stand in the front corner. I'm sure it's the same model I bought at Daddy's Junky Music in Salem, New Hampshire in the 1990s. Then I notice the PA amplifier next to it, which is almost the same exact cheapo Peavey PA as one I bought at Daddy's Junky Music in Salem, New Hampshire in the '90s. This intersection of memory and reality causes me to float from my seat. The guitar is in my hands, and I find myself serenading the backgammon ladies with The Dead Milkmen's "Beach Party Vietnam." I am asked to leave before I get to shout "COS I DON'T HAVE ANY ARMS!" Once I'm outside, I dump my coffee on the sidewalk. I'm not a coffee snob and I'm cheap to boot, so this isn't a choice I make lightly. Normally, I'd suffer through a bad cup of coffee. But not this one.

I walk down Cottage Street to Bliss for a cup of coffee that tastes like coffee, which is a real plus in my book. I order from a woman who, every time I've interacted with her, acts as if she's just received terrible news. Bliss is always empty, which worries me on a selfish level, because it's the best cup of coffee closest to my house. I'm invested in this business succeeding. They have great sandwiches and chili and you should eat here but save me a seat and don't hog the wifi. A rising tide lifts all cups.

A guy sits at a window seat. I immediately dislike him. I'm on guard. His vibe, his energy, his attitude, whatever the fuck you want to call it, is off. Off Guy rates the sandwich he's eating as one of the top three sandwiches he's ever had. He takes off his sneakers. He puts them back on. He mutters "The fuck?" at pretty much nothing. He takes off his camouflage Red Sox hat and puts it back on. He stands up and keeps eating. I sit as still as possible and brace myself. He mumbles and strides out the door, still chewing and drinking. Several minutes later, he returns, bellowing an apology for taking the cup, and reiterating how good his sandwich was, how it hit the spot. I don't know which spot he means specifically, or how hard it was hit, but he is clearly concussed. He growls something almost Godzilla-like and declares "Come on now, wake up!" and storms out to his truck. He's in it and the engine is running and he's doing 30+mph before he's out of the parking space.

I'm still wearing the earflap hat. Wearing a goofy-looking hat is out of my comfort zone. It's like dancing, or wearing colored socks, or telling a waitress she made a mistake on my order. I prefer to fly under the radar, because I incorrectly assume there's a radar, and someone is watching it, and it matters. I sigh a big slow sigh, which means I've taken too long of a lunch break. On the walk home, I pass my brown coffee stain in the snow. "Fuck you," I say.

DEAR YOUNG LADY
WHO DIDN'T LOCK
THE SINGLE-OCCUPANCY
RESTROOM DOOR AT
THE ROOST——

I WILL NOT APOLOGIZE
FOR ACCIDENTALLY
SEEING THE SIDE OF
YOUR BUM, BECAUSE
YOU'RE SUPPOSED TO
LOCK SINGLE-OCCUPANCY
RESTROOM DOORS.

——FROM,
TOM

The Roost: I sit at the big table, nestled between two conversations: To my left, a middle-aged gay man loudly and vividly describes a borderline-inappropriate attempt to seduce a straight guy. I learn a new word: *heteroflexible*. Google tells me there are a quarter of a million results for it, so I'm clearly behind the curve on this one. To my right, two girls West Coast vocal fry at each other. "Mackenzie's daaaad hazn't werked in like, tyeoww yeahrs." "Seth slept weth Jules aaahd I whel halways have thaht to hauld auver heaz head." Their speech transcends normal conversation and enters the realm of amazing comedic minds workshopping characters. I sip my coffee. I always make a little spot on a to-go lid, a barely visible mark left by the tip of my oily Italian nose, a tiny nudge encouraging the plastic to begin its two hundred year journey towards decomposition. We're all headed for the landfill.

CHA-CHING! (BIRD'S STORE, FLORENCE)

I drive to Florence for a haircut. Looking in the barbershop window, I see thousands of people in there waiting. "Shit On That," I declare, and I cross the intersection to Bird's Store. I buy a coffee and a fat little Mead notebook. My coffee is the dregs from two almost-empty coffee pots but it turns out to be pretty good, which is wonderful since I one hundred percent expected it to be terrible. I take a seat at one of the large plastic folding tables marked "Keno-Only." Some old guys are parked there, staring at video screens above the counter. Two are silent screen watchers, the third sighs and mutters a lot. They smell like cigarettes. Our chairs have tennis balls impaled on the feet.

This is an old neighborhood corner store (established 1867, according to the sign on the brick facade) in the heart of Florence center. It has giant windows obscured by assorted crap, tin ceilings high overhead, and a wonderful angled entrance on the corner which is blocked off.

"Thirty-three! Go ahead, tease me!" the mutterer says. "There it is! Cha-ching! That's better!"

We're sitting in a wide aisle between stationary and hardware. The hardware side has everything you might need in a pinch: A pizza slicer which will surely break the first time you use it, a plastic power strip decalled to look like steel plating, and a selection of Leggs Sheer Energy Revitalizing Sheer Pantyhose. An unseen someone in the back of the store greets a friend with a Budweiseresque "WASSSAAAAP!" because that is a thing that still happens on planet Earth in 2016. "All right, let's get going," the mutterer says to the dollar bills in his hand. All right. I head back to the barbershop.

I look through the window again: Three people in the chairs, three more waiting. Not great, but acceptable. I take a seat and sip my coffee and write in my notebook while the Cooking Channel blathers at the room. This barbershop is my biggest exposure to shitty cable television and advertising. *Family Feud* on the Game Show Network. The chick from *Will & Grace* shilling for a skin cream. Authentic Italian spinach dip on the Food Network. Ty Pennington shilling for a mortgage loan website. When I'm in the chair, I get to take off my glasses, which is a blessing. But I still have to listen to the endless stream of bullshit and play along with the barbers' commentary on what's happening on the TV screen, because they have no idea how blind I am.

Mike owns the place. He answers the phone by saying the word "barbershop." It's usually someone asking if the place is open. Sometimes it's someone looking to sign out the Florence Community Room, which Mike is in charge of. He used to have jokes about Obama taped up to his mirror. Before that, he had jokes about Bush. When he cuts my hair, he mumbles semi-dirty jokes I can't hear because there are hair clippers buzzing against my ear. I do my best to imitate how humans laugh.

The self-policing barbershop waiting system fills me with anxiety and worry. Who was before me? Who came in after me? I'm fourth. Fourth, goddamnit! I AM NUMBER FOUR. I assess the speed of the haircuts in progress and conclude I'll get Hue as my barber. She's a nice lady, Thai I think, with a thick accent and a passing acknowledgment of verb tense. I can't understand a goddamned thing she says. My noncommittal hmmm mechanism gets a hell of a workout when she cuts my hair. I'm bad enough at small talk in the best of circumstances. This will kill me. I will die.

There's never any chit-chat between waiting customers here, which is true of most every barbershop I've ever been in. Silent men staring at the TVs or reading newspapers, separated by empty chairs whenever possible, looking straight forward, no eye contact. I slouch in my chair and keep writing and watch Drew Carey's career spiral further into the abyss and wait to get my hair did. All I've got is this cup of coffee and you.

Woodstar Cafe: I sit next to two cute Australian college girls with dyed hair and truly swoon-worthy accents. They show each other Facebook crap on their phones and laugh about Tommy Lee getting stuck on his stupid upside-down drum set. The guy sitting next to me wears a sagging tie-dyed backpack, pajama bottoms, and flip-flops. He has travel books from the library on his table: Cape Cod, Europe, a couple more. I wonder if he'll put on real pants for his big adventure?

AN ODD THING TO DO TO A DEAD MAN (SYLVESTER'S, NORTHAMPTON)

Sunday morning mob scene in the foyer. I excuse-me my way through the waiting breakfast crowd to the cafe side of the building. I order a coffee and a slice of maple apple upside down cake, because I read all of those words on a little card in the glass case, and combined, they sound goddamned delicious.

Sylvester's is the former home of Sylvester Graham, inventor of the graham cracker. Not the most earth-shattering thing to be known for, but here's a restaurant named after him. They sell t-shirts with him on 'em, too. A designer added cartoon aviator sunglasses to an old etching of Sylvester's face. Isn't that an odd thing to do to a dead man?

I sit at one of the three comfy chairs arranged around a tiny little table. A couple sit with me while they wait for an adult-sized table. The wife is going away on a trip, and they're discussing how the husband will eat. He suggests picking up a George Foreman Grill so he can cook chicken. I'm assuming these people live in an average American house with a functional kitchen filled with appliances and pans and so on, but this grown human male thinks he needs to purchase an additional kitchen device, a device endorsed by a man who used to punch things for a living, for greater convenience. "Mark, party of two?" the PA announces. There they go. If they don't get that Foreman grill before Mark's wife goes away, she'll return to find his bloated corpse in the garage, his lips smeared with motor oil. If only he'd had an easy way to cook chicken! Godspeed, Mark.

A little boy spins around in a chair. He's loud and bouncy and little-boyish. His mother hovers nearby, talking with someone, admonishing him every twenty-three seconds or so. She points at me and says to him "Do you see this man? He's reading. Could you be quieter, please?" I've been cast as a Disapproving Adult in someone else's bullshit discipline lesson. The hell? She seems to enjoy squashing the joy out of her boy. Ten straight minutes of

"Sit nicely."
"Off the floor."
"No spinning in the chair."
"You're getting up and down an awful lot."
"Watch the table."

He's crying now. She's more concerned about being

judged by other adults then how her boy feels. She seems like a real fucking asshole.

I sit back in the stupid chair, in the stupid room full of stupid people, because now I'm in a bad mood, so everything is stupid. I pull out my sketchbook and work on the logo for the restaurant that will someday be named after me. I draw my smiling corpse, wearing a noose and crouched on a surfboard. Two-For-One Tuesdays at Pappalardo's Hang Ten Pizza Palace, coming in 2125.

I trudge into town mid-snowstorm. Main Street is unplowed and barely open for business. I seek someone to hand me a cup of coffee in exchange for money, and I find the Haymarket.

We customers hunch over candlelit tables, a damp cross-section of weather-denying Northampton residents. There is an unusual sense of camaraderie here, the strange-but-nice way people can connect when they feel stuck together in a common struggle. A 22News camera crew arrives to capture some Stubborn New Englander footage for their evening broadcast. I sip coffee and eat a banana walnut thing and edit science fiction while a homeless guy snoozes at the next table. When my laptop battery gets cranky, I bundle up and head back out into the bastard cold. My beard freezes under my scarf. My feet are numb. When I get home, I'll light four thousand candles.

SOMETIMES THE MAN IS AWESOME (STARBUCKS, NORTHAMPTON)

The barista's greeting to customers is "What can I start for you?" I like that. It sounds like you're about to embark on a wonderful adventure together. The cynical part of me suspects it's a focus group-approved phrase from the employee manual. I don't frequent these places enough to know for sure. A coffee nerd sits by the order pickup counter, regaling his companions with reverse-French press coffee trivia. He stares lustfully at a fancy machine behind the counter, which is a $9,000 box that Starbucks acquired through a corporate takeover or something. I'd Google it if I cared more, but I get the idea. It's a machine that makes coffee. I step around the nerd's gigantic boner, retrieve my despicably pedestrian black coffee, and sit.

If you're going to sit in a Starbucks and talk about Starbucks and you're me, you're bound to end up talking about the corporate-designed environment. So let's talk about the swell old church pew I'm sitting at. Then we can contrast that with the music I'm hearing on the sound system, which is available for impulse purchase on a counter display near the register. Let's contrast that with the old salvaged doors hanging as wall decoration, and then we can consider the Oprah-branded chai tea latte on the menu board. A Starbucks is a curated experience of strictly regulated uniqueishness.

Starbucks coffee is good. It's a little too caffeinated for my fragile self, but I like it. I have no reason to bother with it in Northampton, because there's better coffee to drink and better places to sit in literally every direction, but I've got nothing against it. I think it's just fine when

I drink it, and I enjoy it most when I'm in a strange town, or Puerto Rico (nothing like the slightest hint of foreignness to make me embrace corporate chains. ¡VIVA FAMILIARIDAD!). Corporate coffee shops also win on the hottest sweltering bastard summer days, when their top-dollar air conditioning kicks the shit out of everybody else's. Sometimes, The Man is awesome.

In the '90s, this was a Coffee Connection. Then one day it was a Starbucks. While some people saw it as a simple takeover, others whispered rumors that it was a tactical move on Starbucks' part, a subterfuge to get a foothold in historically chain-resistant downtown Northampton. I try to fact-check this half-memory online, but my phone browser won't open, so let's just say it's true.

Inoffensive, soft-voiced music floats near the ceiling, an auto-tuned ghost searching for her lost piano notes. I can feel my ears curling up into the fetal position. As my soul dissipates, I am lulled to sleep in the reassuring embrace of the creepy Starbucks logo mermaid. I rally my anger and attempt to focus it on the bullshit rack of travel mugs and the chocolate-covered bullshit in the display case, but it just doesn't seem that important. The rage is no longer in me. There is only Starbucks now. I should just order the Oprah Big Gulp. Dunk my whole fucking head in it. Baptize myself with a bold infusion of cinnamon, ginger, cardamom and cloves until I choke on tea leaves and whatever the fuck rooibos are, and be reborn. This town will crumble to dust but lo, I shall burn bright and infinite with Mermaid Oprah and Starbucks and I think this is too much caffeine for me this late in the day. *O, darkness! O, beast! Main Street is in flames!* I pluck out my eyes and tremble home.

NORTH (SHADY GLEN, TURNERS FALLS)

I'm having a frustrating morning, lots of inner conflict and little things going wrong, things that cause my trip north to feel more challenging than it needs to. I hit my head on my car's hatchback, I'm nursing two or maybe three broken toes from a recent home renovation mishap. I'm not 100% sure of my route but I refuse to consult the internet. I have a headache and my socks feel weird.

It's 10:30 by the time I get to Adam's Donuts in Greenfield. The donut case is almost empty and the seats are filled. This is similar to my previous Adam's visits. Someday, I'll make it here and there'll be actual donuts to put in my actual mouth.

I continue north. I miss breakfast at the Wagon Wheel in Gill by twenty lousy minutes, so I cross the bridge and swing into Shady Glen's parking lot. Shady Glen: the place that sounds like it was named after your step-dad's drinking buddy. An old woman whacks her SUV door into my side mirror. No apology. I limp inside, overwhelmed by the eye-piercing psychotic yellow counter and tables. My coffee is delivered in a big heavy mug. I own one and use it every morning at home. My breakfast arrives promptly and my morning becomes less terrible. Pancake redemption!

I steal a pen from the counter to write this. I'm a man who always has multiple ballpoint pens on his person, so of course I don't have one this morning, this morning of sixty tiny failures and forty minor defeats. I rub my head. Goddamned hatchback.

There's a small toy model of a diner on the counter,

with a "Please don't touch" sign next to it. A little boy touches it. "Don't touch it, Devin," his dad warns as he pays the bill. Devin touches it again. That's just Devin's way. I check the time on my phone, but the screen has frozen, because of course it has. I tip well and take the pen.

SHELTER NOHO

Downtown Northampton has been struggling recently, so I was glad to hear one of our town's many vacant storefronts had finally been filled, and by a new cafe no less! Now, I'm no fan of gimmicky restaurants, but how could I *not* stop in? How could I not have a cup of coffee at New England's first (and possibly last) homeless-themed cafe?

I walk into the crooked brick building next to the police station. Shelter Noho has remodeled the place, though 'demodeled' might be a more suitable term. Cardboard boxes fill the corners, with garbage artfully strewn across the floor. Wooden pallets serve as tabletops, balanced on trash barrels. Customers lounge in rusted lawn chairs. In the back corner, there's a filthy pup tent I have absolutely no desire to look in.

The centerpiece of the room is a steel drum with a fake fire in it — fluttering red and orange paper streamers lit from below and blown by a hidden fan. I circle around it, ignoring two hobos asking me if I have any spare change, and order my coffee from a young woman wearing a trash bag. The barista next to her balances a bindle on his shoulder as he pours a perfect image of a shopping cart in latte foam. My $6 single-source pour-over coffee comes in a used styrofoam cup. In an old soup can near the creamers, sugar packets are hidden amongst crack vials and empty Fireball nip bottles. Forks and spoons stick out of a worn-out boot, mingling with dirty syringes and cigarette butts. I assume these are all props, but at this point I don't know what to think.

Near the intentionally overflowing trash cans by the front window, customers are encouraged to sit on stacked milk crates and put their feet up on homeless people. Yes, that's right. Real local homeless people are being paid to be footstools for the more fortunate. Shelter Noho's Facebook page insists this is an innovative program for getting these folks back into the workforce. One of these 'featured guests,' a fellow named Harold, cries tears of shame, hunched under the vintage Pumas of a young man remixing a song on his iPad. Harold served in the first Iraq war, he tells me. He's doing this, he says, to try and get back on his feet. There's a joke in there, but I don't have the heart to make it come out of my mouth. A girl kneels down next to him and takes a selfie. This is what our town has turned into, this is what our culture has produced. Where are the protesters? Where's the outrage? I have no words. I usually have words.

Honestly, though, it's a great cup of coffee.

SALVATION A LA MODE
(SMITH STUDENT CENTER CAFE, NORTHAMPTON)

I walk up the hill to Smith College and order a small iced coffee and a slice of pizza from the Smith Student Center Cafe. My straw is 2.5 times taller than my cup, which makes me feel foolish. The pizza is room temperature but tasty. Somebody is outside giving away free ice cream, but I'm too self-conscious to go out and ask if it's open to the public or not. A cameraman films the whole event, because clearly, this needs to be documented. I'm one of the only non-employee dudes in this large, loud concrete-floored room, and I feel like a trespasser. But I'll tolerate a lot of anxiety for cheap, decent pizza.

Lots of girls lying on the lawn in the sun. I'm grateful I grew up and stopped being attracted to college-aged girls. In my twenties, I'd harbored a fear that maybe I'd grow up to be a lecherous creep, a nerdy Aqualung. Only a certain kind of 20-year old guy worries about this sort of thing.

I want some goddamned free ice cream. Don't I deserve free ice cream? What's stopping me from walking up to the table and asking for some free ice cream? What's the worst thing that could happen? An *Invasion Of the Body Snatchers*-style pointing and shrieking by the entire campus while the cameraman captures it all and posts it to YouTube? Okay, Tom. Fair point. That is actually the worst thing that could happen.

The Roost: I watch a girl sitting in the soft serve shop's window seat across the street, who is watching me sitting in the coffee shop's window seat across the street. A few tables away, a twenty-something explains to her friends how BMWs are *nice*, but not *really* luxury cars. I want to hit her with a Mercedes S Class. A woman walks in with a large iced coffee from Panera, which is bad form in general, and gross in this specific case, because that coffee is for shit. Three college kids sit at the big table with me, joking about how to pronounce "Worcester" in a New England accent. I roll my eyes so far back I can read the tag on my shirt. Fahkin outtastatahs.

IN THE NEIGHBORHOOD

I attempt to drink coffee and walk. This might sound like a simple task, but I prove to be deceptively simpler. I'm housebound on a warm February afternoon, twenty-four hours into a sinus headache, which saps my willingness to move from wherever I am. It's past 3 o'clock on a Sunday in Easthampton, Massachusetts, which diminishes walkable coffee options by 98%. I challenge myself to crawl off the couch, Advil up, brew some goddamn coffee, and enjoy the weather. A true underdog, I rise to meet my own challenge. Four scoops of coffee grounds later, I'm walking up my street with a coffee mug.

It is not a travel mug, unfortunately, just a regular mug-mug. A stationary mug? A home mug. It's not designed for this walking business, or maybe *I'm* not, because I'm spilling hot coffee all over my hand. I walk up one street and down another. Porches are wrapped in plastic, holdout snow clings to the sidewalks. My mug is half empty and I'm somehow still spilling it. Do I walk funny? Am I a loper? I don't know. I need some sort of Steadicam rig for coffee. A SteadiCup.

I circle back towards home earlier than planned. The air and the movement help with the sinus pain a bit, or maybe it's the caffeine, or the ibuprofin, or being upright. Whatever it is, I still don't feel that great, and I'm exhausted, sort of bored, and damp-handed. I walk past my neighbor's house. It has one of those spinning attic vent things on the roof. The turbine has a bad bearing and clicks. A little kid and his dad emerge from a nearby condo complex. The boy steers a toy four-wheeler, travelling approximately slower-than-walking-MPH. He wears a helmet, in case he's suddenly overtaken by a malevolent tailwind.

I approach my house, a three-story to-do list. I pass the corpse of a sapling I transplanted and accidentally killed (sorry, little dude). In my screen porch, things have been thoroughly mussed by winter winds. Shoulda wrapped it in plastic, I guess. I step over a pile of scrap wood and drop into a bench seat liberated from an Econoline van. It has seat belts and little ashtrays built into the armrests and everything. Without warning, the clouds part and God's hand reaches down from the heavens to spill my coffee one last time. I will clean it up in two months. Now that I've acknowledged the clicking sound from my neighbor's roof, I realize I can hear it from my porch. It shall taint every yard-based activity from now until my death. It shall haunt my nights. It's going to be a long spring.

Woodstar Cafe: Two conservative college kids commiserate, sharing stories of their outlandishly liberal peers, prefacing every poorly-constructed straw man argument with an "I KNOW, RIGHT?" They talk about riots and race for a solid ten minutes, and successfully avoiding any mention of human beings at all, focusing solely on laws and property. This is a rare local sighting, these young hawks. Their Banana Republic plumage is breathtaking this time of year.

PAPER OR PLASTIC?
(C@FE HADLEY AT STOP & SHOP, HADLEY)

I hunch in the corner of C@fe Hadley, the quirky funky little indie coffeeshop nestled next to the checkout area of the Stop & Shop on Route 9. Ha-ha-ha. Just kidding. It's an alcove with a few tables shoved into it. But since supermarket management has the audacity to bestow this space with a stupid name and a stupid sign, I muster the audacity to sit here and drink coffee.

My coffee is made and served by a coin-operated machine in the bakery department. I tap the touchscreen, a progress bar fills in, and *voilà!* Warm brown water in a cup. It tastes exactly how you might suspect an emotionless automaton might think coffee might taste.

I sit amongst jugs of Poland Spring Water, a Megabucks kiosk, and a locked case of infant formula. A wall is decorated with nine identical images of the American flag, eight black and white, one in color. These colors don't run one out of nine times. My robot juice is godawful. I chew on an apple turnover I bought in the bakery department. It's like eating a small backpack coated in sugar. No one else pauses to sit here and no one looks at me. I fade to floor tile beige, losing permanence, and I'm gone.

> "If you're dead, you don't feel anything. That's what I've been told."
> – Old guy to another old guy, Dunkin Donuts

133

HAZY COSMIC JIVE
(BRASS BUCKLE, GREENFIELD)

The Brass Buckle is one of those rare small businesses where the owners display their nerd/scifi fandom proudly. It's just not that often you see a restaurant decorated with *Firefly* posters. A painted moonscape awaits you on the bathroom door. The walls are adorned with framed comic book pages: *Star Wars, Hellboy, Wolverine.* "Fuck this and fuck that!" Johnny Rotten howls out of the stereo. I appreciate a good bit of cussing with my breakfast. I order the corned beef hash — more food than I eat in a day, sometimes. I don't mind because it's goddamned delicious. It distracts me from writing, and now my plate is empty. Jesus, did I just eat that? Jesus says yes.

Bowie's "Starman" plays on the stereo, which was the exact song rocking out of my car speakers when I parked on Main Street. It's been a few weeks since Mr. Bowie's death, and he's still on my mind. I don't tend to get emotional about people who I don't know (...or *do* know, *am I right, pals?!?!?*), but I find myself dwelling on this particular celebrity death more than usual. Like Joe Strummer, Phil Hartman, and Adam Yauch, sometimes these losses cut deeper than I anticipate. So I've been spinning Bowie's records and watching live clips on YouTube. David Bowie has left us important homework: Listen to David Bowie.

> ## "The stars were doing weird things."
> *– Hippie dude talking about being high in the woods, The Haymarket*

Tandem Bagel: Sitting in the cafe's patio area, I enjoy the hell out of a coffee and a bagel. Four small birds eye me from under the next table. I keep my hands moving, staking a claim on my table, its contents, and the airspace above it. "Jackals," I mutter. The chubby birds tilt their heads and hop closer. "Adorable jackals." I realize I can't picture what a jackal actually looks like. I can conjure a vague image from maybe a Disney cartoon, but that's it. They're like, bad dogs, right? There's a part of my mind which is already composing this self-deprecating observation into a tweet, packaging it for consumption. This is a terrible thing I do.

CAFE OR NOT CAFE
(FREEDOM CAFE, AMHERST)

I crawl the gauntlet of North Pleasant Street, rolling through the heart of the UMASS Amherst campus in first gear. It is a rainy Wednesday afternoon with terrible visibility. Two thousand drenched twenty-somethings fail to look up as they squish cross the five hundred crosswalks before me.

I park in the squishy driveway of The Freedom Cafe, a student activist-run cafe on the far edge of campus. Their Facebook page describes their fundraising efforts to fight slavery. What their Facebook page *doesn't* describe is the cafe itself, which isn't a cafe at all. It's a walk-up counter. I jog in out of the rain, dripping wet, muddy shoes, laptop bag and to-do list in tow. There is no place to sit. I find myself somewhere between bummed out and annoyed. But the workers are earnest volunteer kids, so I don't want to be all WHADDAYA MEAN NO GODDAMNED TABLES AND CHAIRS. No one wants to hear me break down the meaning of the word "cafe" and all that it implies to the consumer. No one. So I order a cup of pour-over to-go, because it seems too awkward to just turn around and leave. I listen to the slavery spiel (sex trafficking in India), and I'm encouraged to donate what I want in exchange for the coffee, by putting money in a jar and taking whatever change I want. I hate that sort of transaction, so I just throw in a five. The pour-over is meticulously pored over. The pouring takes a supernaturally long time. I mean, wow.

One stilted conversation later, I'm drinking a $5 cup of coffee in my Ford Focus, three towns away from home, wet, and still in possession of work that needs doing. The coffee, it turns out, is really good. I sit and listen to the rain hitting the car roof. It's a lovely sound, a sound that almost makes the trip worth it, aside from the fact that I could've made a coffee in my kitchen and sat in my car in my driveway. I start the engine. I guess I need to go get a cup of coffee somewhere?

The Roost: It's quiet here. The post office was quiet, too. It makes me wonder if something terrible has happened, that I'm missing a dire local or world event. Or maybe it's Rapture Time. I could look it up on my phone, but I don't. Outside, a couple lock up their bikes to the light pole. The woman takes a photo of this activity, to keep her social sphere up-to-date on her whereabouts and activities. My caption guess: "SUMMER, Y'ALL!! #summer #newengland #outofshape." A few tables away, a man laughs at something his wife says. It's a loud, too-long Horshack type of laugh, accompanied by an open-palm table-slap. It's the most insincere thing I've heard in months.

PINE STREET CAFE (FLORENCE)

I think the Pine Street Cafe is a new business, but it turns out to be a rebranded Sunrise Over Florence Cafe. Owner change, name change, same menu, same weird chairs. A handwritten sign on the door asks patrons to please visit their website, to help with their Google rating. This — I'm pretty sure — is not a thing. Unless maybe it's

2003 or something?

I order a coffee and a dense slab of apple pie roll. It's a three-something dollar item I've never heard of before, and immediately love. For five dollars, I could've upgraded to a mini-pie, but I think I show nigh-heroic restraint in my choice. I sit and write and fret about money. I fret about money because I'm self-employed. I fret about money because it's April and I just came from my tax preparer's office. Days like this are stuffed full of self-doubt, a pastry of worry fruit squeezed between flaky layers of second-guessing, topped with raw panic sugar. I fork off another cube and place it on my tongue. This isn't the healthiest lunch choice, but it's tasty as fuck, and I'm up two bucks because of that no-mini-pie decision. I'm practically making money right now, baby.

Woodstar Cafe: I can see up a young lady's skirt. I'm not particularly interested in looking up her skirt, on a sexual attraction or even a regular-old curiosity level, but there's this line-of-sight thing happening, making the view difficult to avoid if my eyes are open. So I'm writing this paragraph instead. It's not a particularly interesting paragraph, but it's keeping my eyes on my laptop screen right in this moment, so in that sense it's a pretty good paragraph, or functionally useful at the very least. Gosh, this blueberry muffin is good. Say, how about those Red Sox base-of-ball players? What's up with gas stations charging 9/10ths of a penny, anyhow? My, the weather is so inclemental today! This paragraph deserves a goddamned award.

SLICE AND A CUP
(SAM'S PIZZERIA & CAFE, NORTHAMPTON)

Most pizza places don't have good coffee. Most cafes don't offer pizza. Neither one is rocket science, and both are popular items, but somehow you just don't see them paired together often. And when you do see them combined, it's sometimes seems a bit weird. But Sam's makes it work. They do it right. Good coffee, good pizza. Not weird.

A dog barks, echoing through the U-shaped double storefront. There always seems to be a dog in here. I sip my coffee, and when my cheeseburger-something-thingamajig slice is ready, a pretty girl brings it to my table. Someone taps a few keys on the piano in the corner, which triggers an instant fight-or-flight response in me. A big guy walks in, a truly giant dude. Easily two and a half Toms wide, here is a man who dominates every space he enters. He watches a video with his phone volume all the way up and bellows things to his friends. Doesn't give a shit. I wonder what he drives. The dog barks and his owner allatrates a reply, causing me to shoehorn in an odd vocabulary word, which is a favorite pastime of mine. My phone automatically connects to Sam's wifi, even though I don't think I've been here in over a year, and I've only owned this phone for six months. AM I BEING HACKED.

I remember when this storefront was a Quizno's. Before that, it was Bart's Homemade Ice Cream, with their hideous wall art. In between those businesses, it was Not-Bart's-Homemade-Ice-Cream, a short stint where the owner and the franchisee had a dispute, which caused the whole deal to fall apart. I painted a tabletop for that place.

It got sold off when they closed, and sat outside Lucky's Tattoos for a few years, until the elements and leaning smokers took their toll, and then it fell apart, too.

"GoodafternoonwelcometoBliss!!!!!" the energetic young man behind the counter calls across an expanse of empty restaurant, before my body is fully through the door. It's an aggressive assault of faux-friendly customer service I can barely tolerate. I smile, which the outside world sees as a death-mask grimace, something carved into trees to warn travelers of unholy ground. I don't photograph well.

EARLY-ASS-O'CLOCK
(JOHNNY'S ROADSIDE DINER, HADLEY)

Johnny's Roadside Diner is a pre-fab diner built in the late 1990s, designed to mimic an idealized 1970s pop culture version of the 1950s. It is pseudo-retro: Lots of polished stainless steel, chrome-looking plastic light fixtures and trim, with pink and blue neon tubes running throughout the two dining rooms. Everything is too bright and fluorescent for my should-be-sleeping eyes to handle. Even the shadows are well-lit.

I'm sitting at a counter stool at early-ass-o'clock in the morning, after a sleepless night and a strong desire for egg yolk. Four old guys meet up in the booth behind me, regulars who cover topics ranging from hockey to America's crumbling infrastructure to Ebola, all in the first five minutes of shit-shooting. One guy compliments my leather jacket, but I don't realize he's talking to me at first. I apologize, saying I only half-heard him, and he asks me which half. Get a load of Henny Youngman over here.

Spaces like this are pretend-places. They're mini-theme parks that chip away at my soul. I understand all buildings require an amount of artifice, or you'd be looking at insulation and wiring wherever you went. But this stuff actually *offends* me. I don't say that happily or proudly. It's goddamned tiring, the relentless opinion-having, observation-making, the energy I expend mounting arguments in my head. Maybe I just can't stand easily-washable surfaces, I don't know. The food is fine. The workers seem fine. Why can't I just enjoy myself at a place like this? Everyone else here seems to enjoy it, and I'm pulling this phony Holden Caulfield bullshit all the time.

I need to wake up. I need to meditate on this cup of coffee and wake up. It's not a bad cup of coffee or anything. Just drink the coffee, Tom. Just drink the fucking coffee.

> I sit in the window of Greenfield Coffee, editing this book for what feels like the fifty-fuckieth time, as jazzy trumpets twoot at the back of my head. What's with jazz and coffee shops? How about an old Bob Newhart record? Nature sounds? An idling diesel engine? Gunfire? Anything but these swinging zim-zams and brassy bwap-bwaps. Anything.

LUCK OF THE IRISH
(WHOLE DONUT, HOLYOKE)

A handwritten sign on the door says "CASH ONLY." Taped to the counter, another sign says "CASH ONLY," and on the cash register, there's a helpful and informative sign announcing "CASH ONLY." A group of loud young-people-I-immediately-dislike barge through the door, all dressed in green. High school? College? I can't even tell anymore. I could give a shit. The boys speak with exaggerated New England accents, really hamming it the fuck up, in my eastern Mass opinion.

"KENWE YOUSE YAW BATHRUM?"
"DOOYA GODDA BUYA DOH-NUT?"

One of the guys waits with a girl by the counter while their friends pee and poop without buying doh-nuts. "We met last night," the girl says to him. "Do you remember my name?" He does not. Haddaya like them apples.

I order a small black coffee and a jelly stick. Well, the little sign in the glass case says they're called Jellystix, but I'm not sure if that's singular or plural. There's no music playing, so aside from the refrigerator case, all I can hear is my notebook grinding sugar granules into the tabletop. "Hi, Colleeeeeeeen!" a man coos at the counter woman as he pushes through the door. In one breath, he says "You wallpapered. I got laid off. Fuckin' assholes." Colleeeeeeen says nothing.

Outside, cops mill around the intersection, and I notice more people wearing green clothes. Irish pride shit. I realize I've stumbled into a road race, The Holyoke Saint Patrick's 10K. Engine 5 pulls into the Whole Donut lot as crowds form along the street to watch other people run, which is a thing to do, I guess. The one goddamned day I drive into goddamned Holyoke for a goddamned donut and coffee, and I've put myself on a goddamned race course. Ugh. My car's going to get blocked in this parking lot and I'll be trapped in a shamrock-infested hellscape for hours.

Fuck this. I scrawl a number on my shirt with the remains of my Jellystix and sprint out the door. The crowd cheers me as I pass. "CASH ONLY!" they chant. "CASH ONLY!" I run, arms spread, flipping off both sides of the street. It only causes them to cheer more. I run and I run, to a place where the weekend leprechauns can't catch me, to a place where I can be free.

POSTSCRIPT

NOT LOOKING DOWN THE BARREL OF A GUN

(DUNKIN DONUTS, HAVERHILL)

It was a quiet exchange, and the customers didn't even realize anything had happened until the guy with the gun had run out the door, crossed the parking lot, jumped a guardrail, and disappeared into the woods. Then the cashier started bawling her eyes out, and we all caught on. I'd been sitting in a Dunkin Donuts booth with my friend Mark in Haverhill, Massachusetts, my hometown. It was the mid-1990s, sometime around midnight, and the place had just been robbed.

The natural order of doughnut-serving, doughnut-purchasing, and doughnut-consuming broke down immediately. The cashier cried on the shoulder of her shift manager, who was trying to talk to the cops on the phone. We customers peered out into the night, trying to see past our own fluorescent-lit reflections, trying to see where the gun dude had run off to. This hubbub was punctuated by the squawking, tinny voices of irate customers chattering over the unmanned drive-thru intercom.

I was tempted to jump over the counter and take command of the drive-thru, to fill their orders, to keep my fellow New Englanders properly lubricated with jelly and caffeine. But I resisted that temptation, because Haverhill boasted at least 12 other Dunkin Donuts locations, so it's not like they couldn't go drive-thru somewhere else.

At the next booth, a high school girl convinced herself that she had just barely escaped disaster. She announced to the room, "Awmagaad! I coulda gawt shot!" She repeated this several times, her panic and volume increasing with each iteration, as she looked to her boyfriend for confirmation that, yes, indeed, awmagaad, she coulda gawt shot. I could guess what was running through her head: "OH MY GAWD. THERE'S SOMETHIN HAPPENIN AROUND ME THAT SEEMS LIKE SOMETHIN ON TV. I HAVE SOMETHIN TO TALK ABOUT IN HOMEROOM TOMORROW. O MY GAWD." She was trying as hard as she could to turn this into some sort of Defining Life Experience. She eventually interrogated the still-crying cashier for details: What was it like? Were you scared? Did you see the gun? Awmagaad. Each response was memorized for the following day's five minute passing period between Algebra and Biology. This girl was determined to remember every moment of this dramatic episode in her life, especially the ones that didn't happen to her.

In fact, this girl decided she was *so* traumatized, *so* endangered, she had to go outside to the payphone and call her mother to tell her how distraught she was over the gun-toting dude who had just run across the parking lot, jumped the guardrail, and disappeared into the woods. The problem I have with this clever course of action is—okay, yeah, fine, call your mom—But the payphone is *outside. Across the parking lot. Over by the guardrail. Right next to the woods.*

NOTES

• This book is the culmination of a two-year journal project. I wrote it as a way to motivate myself, to push my recently-divorced ass out my apartment door and keep me among human beings. It also proved to be a fine writing prompt, a good exercise in mindfulness: Go to a place. Sit. Listen. It mostly worked.

• I'd like to express half-a-ton of respect to the fine local establishments who, every damned day, put up with an endless stream of customers like myself (and ones who are much, much worse). Let's observe a moment of silence for the businesses who have closed between the writing and publishing of these words: Sip, Look Restaurant, Dunkin Donuts (Main Street, Northampton), The Foundry (ceased being a coffeehouse), Sunrise Over Florence Cafe (reopened as Pine Street Cafe), The Yellow Sofa, Faces Cafe, Bliss (damn it!), and Dusty Rose's Creamery.

My acknowledgment of these closings in no way implies any wrongdoing on my part. Or maybe it does, I don't know. Ain't nobody getting rich selling small cups of black coffee. Businesses need business to stay in business. Make sure you support the ones you like.

• Two entries in this book were April Fool's jokes. The postscript, *Not Looking Down The Barrel Of A Gun*, is a story I wrote in the early aughts, a sort of proto-*1MCOC*. I decided to include it in this collection, as it fits nicely and I still like it.

• The word "coffee" appears two hundred and twenty-three times in this book. "Fuck," forty-two times. "Shit," forty-nine times. "Poop," five times. "Hellscape," appears twice, but it *feels* like it's in there more, know what I mean?

• The title of this book (and the Facebook page that preceded it) is a pop culture reference, a thing I normally avoid, but damned if it didn't *fit*. I think it's a pretty good song, as long as Bob Dylan isn't singing it.

• I spent an unreasonable amount of time debating the use of "cafe" versus "café." Apparently usage of "cafe" is overtaking the non-Anglicized word, but I still sort of feel like I'm typing a mistake. On the other hand, as an American who eschews all things Fancy, I feel like the diacritic draws undue attention to itself and prods the inner voice towards over-enunciation. *Oh, my! He's at a café! Par-doan mwaah!* Maybe I overthink these things. Generally, I prefer "coffee shop." Ugh, but then there's that shit Red Hot Chili Peppers song... *Fuuuuuck.*

• This is a self-published book, meaning it was lovingly created and dropped into an indifferent black hole of non-distribution and slight promotion. Consider writing a brief review on Amazon, Goodreads, wherever. Word-of-mouth is crucial and I'd love to bask in your scathing critiques.

• Many thanks to Jon Bartlett, Josh Gilb, Mark Reusch, Matt Smith, and Dana Wilde for their invaluable proofreading and feedbacking.

COFFEE POSTERS & PRINTS!

Screenprinted art prints, vinyl stickers, & digital posters.
More info at **tompappalardo.com**

Everything You Didn't Ask For:
Comics and Stories by Tom Pappalardo
164 pages. 10"x7"
Available at **tompappalardo.com** and **amazon.com**

Tom Pappalardo is a graphic designer,
writer, cartoonist, and musician. He lives
in Western Massachusetts with a little cat
named Charlie.

———

TOMPAPPALARDO.COM

Made in the USA
Middletown, DE
29 September 2017